Grace

Awakening

Essence

by Diadra Price

Grace Awakening Essence
Author: Diadra Price
Copyright 2005 ~ Diadra Price

BODY, MIND & SPIRIT / Mental & Spiritual Healing /
Metaphysical

BookSurge Publishing 2005

BOOKSURGE P U B L I S H I N G

To order additional copies, please contact:
BookSurge, LLC
www.booksurge.com
1-866-308-6235
orders@booksurge.com
Cover photo by Jim DeLutes, www.jdlphotos.com
Graphics by Angel Gates
Chalice of the Heart, art by Lyrea Crawford

ISBN# 1-887884-17-3

Dedication

This book is dedicated to my beloved husband, John A. Price, whose Essence has been my greatest gift of Grace. In his eyes I have been able to see the unconditional love of God. In his arms I have felt the cocoon of safety during my transformation. In his voice I have heard the call of the Divine, whispering the promise kept of my dreams come true. In his presence I have known the Beloved, and I have been set free to Love.

Words of endearment and gratitude to these beloved souls. Without them this presentation of Grace Awakening Essence would never have made it into the written word.

Angel Gates ~ the precious expression of love, wisdom, and kindness, devoted assistant

Pat Bellamy ~ the benevolent voice of support, the hands of service, a wonderful teacher

Jere Hand ~ the mirror of unconditional love and virgin innocence, a friend for eternal life

Bob & Janice Carter ~ the gifts of Grace, the dream keepers, the miracle minded voices of faith

October Craig ~ the selfless service, eyes of love and wisdom to the written word

Light Roper ~ the devoted one, the love, wisdom, and livingness of truth to life

Beth Humphrey ~ the gentle Spirit, passionate heart, servant of truth, and voice of wisdom

Victoria Bradley ~ the heart of God, fulfillment of Grace and truth, my beloved sister, soul mate of joy

Dawn Wickham ~ the light of my life, my precious daughter who makes my heart sing

Table of Contents

Introduction

Grace Awakening Essence

By Diadra Price

This book was written for the miracle minded, those
who already believe. It was written for you whose intellectual
pursuits no longer satisfy the hunger and thirst of your soul. It
was not written to convince, persuade, or change your mind,
but to validate and support that which is emerging from the
Essence of your Being. Much of what you encounter here will
appeal to the highly developed reasoning of your mind, but
more importantly, it will quicken your mind of Grace that is far
beyond reasoning. These words of Grace, herein absorbed by the
scan of your eye and I, will call forth the seed code of the Word
of Grace that rests eternally within your soul. Impassioned from
the Essence of your Being, your hunger and thirst for truth can
only be satisfied by this living Word revealed.

Confirmation of something stirring deeply within the heart
of your soul is now your motivation to know, and you have
arrived at the portal of shifting desires—shifting from the desire
to learn and grow to the desire to know and flow. You will soon
stand before the mirror of your Self in wonder and in awe, if you
are not doing that already. Your intellect will intuitively rest as
your Gracemind takes its destined place upon the throne of your
awareness to make all things new. From these words forward
you will not be taught but unfolded and remembered.

This is not a book of knowledge or speculation but of
wisdom and love gathered from *your heart* as the truth that
sets you free. Hope will not be found here, for hope always
leaves room for doubt. Hope is exchanged for knowing. Belief is
exchanged for the known. Speculation is exchanged for truth, for
in the living Word of Grace you already know the truth in which
your freedom rests. Nothing in this book can be proved, for just
as the proof of the pudding is in the eating, the 'proof' of truth is

in its fruits. Truth is realized and recognized, not analyzed! Such is Grace awakening.

The Essence of Grace consciousness is not observable. Therefore, any attempt on my part to define this ineffable consciousness is somewhat limited, for to do so generates content in your mind. You may ask, "Why do it?" I do it because *words of truth always point in the direction of the essence of what is being described. If followed, the truth contained within the descriptive words will awaken to mind the essence of that to which they point.*

God rests in the infinite and plays in the finite. Somewhere within these extremes you now find yourself emerging. True to the nature of God, these two polar extremes call you in equal measure. Your Spirit that knows itself as the Essence of God (the eternal 'I') seeks conscious memory of rest in the infinity of God as well as play in the finite world of creation. Synthesized, these two polar extremes are emerging as a life lived from the fulfillment of Grace consciousness expressing as you. In this state, miracles become the norm. Your true nature of Peace, Love, and Joy impulses your creative processes, and your creations mirror original design. In awe, you, the spiritual human, are emerging like a butterfly, as something completely 'other,' set free by the living Word of Grace written in your heart.

As Gracemind continues to awaken, you will find that doing and being merge, question and answer become one, and time and eternity rest in each other's arms as soul mates of eternal life. All paradoxes are reconciled; the journey and the destination are both means to new beginnings; extremes meet and are but finite expressions of one thing. The explained is defined by the unexplained, the known is made possible through the unknown, and the All is One. In this wisdom, Gracemind in you and me returns home and lives in the world *accepting* the All, while at the same time *changing* all things to reflect the Mind from which the All emerged.

And now as you enter into these words of Grace, may you be ever mind-full of God emerging as re-membered union in your awareness. Union is already a given. Realization of union simply awaits your acceptance to be remembered. Grace is at work in you now and makes itself known through your intention to remember, your intention to glorify God, and your willingness to stay present in awe and wonder. The Word you are holding in your hand is holding you. It is written in your heart and will be made flesh. The truth of it will set you free, and you will recognize the truth by its fruits.

"The winds of Grace blow all the time.

All we need to do is set our sails"

Ramakrishna

"Spirit is in a state of Grace forever.

Your reality is only spirit.

Therefore you are in a state of Grace forever."

A Course In Miracles T-1 ... III 5:4

Section I

Grace Awakening

Chapter One

The Yearning

Chapter 1

The Yearning

I believe in butterflies ... and the metaphor for which they stand.
But, in a space between two worlds I sit ...
Attached to my cocoon by a single strand.
I know I am free, but my wings cannot seem to fly.

In a space between two worlds I sit like a butterfly caught ever so slightly, but tightly in the remnant of my opened cocoon. I am not the caterpillar I once thought myself to be, crawling in the dust of the earth. I can see myself—my beautiful Self—the one I knew all along was contained inside. I remember the many feet I had and the many steps I took to travel even a short distance in the earth. But now I can see my wings and feel the power inside to fly—to fly free above the earth and travel far and wide. I am not what I once thought myself to be; I am free. I really, truly am, except for this one seemingly heavy thread that keeps me attached to my opened cocoon. How can one thread of this womb of sleep that kept me safe in rest, surrendered to the Will of God, now become the binding rope of attachment that keeps me from the new freedom I know and feel?

I can remember when it began to spin, and spin and spin again,
until the darkness overcame my sight,
and I felt myself drawn within—into a long and very dark night.

The metamorphosis of the butterfly has always been my favorite analogy of spiritual awakening. In the human Spirit it is something that might be correlated to ascension. I see ascension as a process of moving from one awareness in consciousness to another. Finally, we ascend to the level of eternal life consciousness wherein we become a new creature in Christ, set free to be all we are created to be. I don't see ascension as an actual physical thing at this point of our evolution, although the physical always reflects our inner states of awareness in due time, or should I say, 'in no time at all.'

I see Christ, and every other truly enlightened teacher, as the exemplified Essence of Being, or the Light of every soul—*"The true light that enlightens every man ..."* (John 1:9) When enough of us are focused and functioning from the deeper levels of our spiritual DNA (Divine Nature Attributes), we will be in a position for a possible collective consciousness raising. Then we will ascend collectively, as carnal mind experiences a transmutation into the more expanded depths of Gracemind. This is true transformation which will affect/effect a quantum leap in the awakening of the whole. When this happens, we will become something completely 'other,' as in the analogy of the caterpillar awakening to the butterfly within. This is what I believe to be the mystical meaning of ascension and the explanation of what is now taking place within us all.

Ascension has become a household-friendly buzz word of the New Age. But, Beloved, we have ascended beyond the New Age into the Age of Grace—an age of metamorphosis of the soul emerging from Essence by the power of ineffable Love. Welcome to the finish line for this stage of our evolution. From here we do not go on alone or on our own. We ascend together, for in truth All is One. There is only *One* who enters the kingdom of heaven. There is only *One* who becomes truly enlightened. Ascension is happening to everyone, regardless of religious persuasion; it is happening to the atheist and the guru alike. It is happening in worlds beyond this one, for it is a natural expansion of the evolution of the infinite potentiality of the All in its original design.

We are ascending through a consciousness shift into Grace awareness functioning within us as Gracemind. *Gracemind* is the frequency of Light serving as the magnetic field of attraction at the center of our Being. It is the consciousness of the Divine which draws and absorbs the darkness into itself, emerging as something totally other. Grace is the power uniting the universe and the spiritual glue holding the children of God in eternal life. *Gracemind* is the master key to all of the doors of the many mansions in God's universe. It is the ascending force of Love.

Ascension is not measurable by traditional geometric methods; it can be measured only by the degree of love oozing from us for absolutely no reason. Effortlessly expressed, unconditional in nature, Gracemind reveals our Divine nature. In all of life's activities—in our attitudes, in our family and all relationships, in our ability to cope with what life offers— unconditional love is the only barometer of our ascension into Gracemind awareness.

In this pilgrimage of Grace we will examine the gradual awakening of Gracemind in the soul. We will see that this awakening is the process of ascension taking place as a natural phenomenon of our destiny. We will first examine our yearnings and heart's desires to determine how they serve this purpose. In the chapter titled *The Gracing*, we will come to view our spiritual inheritance as the gifts of Gracemind already given.

We will look deeply into a new definition of the word, 'truth' to recognize it as part of the matrix of our Divine inheritance. We will see how truth functions as spiritual law in the creative processes of consciousness.

We will explore the shifting awareness of our mind and heart as expansion in Gracemind calls us through portals of awareness not yet recognized. We will see with spiritual vision that the role of surrender is the most empowering activity of *acceptance* within the journey of awakening.

We will also explore the mindsets of the prodigal caterpillar in the evolutionary steps and stages it encounters during the earthly journey of Grace awakening. We will examine the content of the conscious and subconscious levels of mind that keeps us stuck in karma.

In our study together, we will come to recognize and welcome the so called, 'dark night of the soul,' seeing it as the silken threads of Grace enfolding us in a cocoon of protection as the fear of annihilation and sense of separation from God are extinguished. We will examine the many threads that form the cocoon of our final metamorphosis. Ultimately, we will discover how to disconnect the single thread that seems to keep us from spreading our wings in our new found unbounded freedom of Grace.

The Story of My Yearning

I came into the world adoring Jesus, loving him from the beginning, so much so it was an obsession, even as a toddler. I was drawn to his pictures, recognizing him instantly though each portrait was uniquely different. This unaccountable love for Jesus grew with time and expanded into a life-long passion to understand his teachings. I yearned for a personal experience and relationship with him, but settled for the companionship of his message. *The Gospel According to John (RSV)* became my favorite of his words, though I didn't understand why I liked that gospel more than the others. I would read and reread it—it would be several decades later before I understood the reason. I came to affectionately call it *The Book of Love.*

In addition to my love for Jesus and his message, there was an unexplainable passion for truth that reached volcanic intensities. So much of what I was exposed to as a child in religious settings seemed contradictory. I hungered and thirsted for truth. My heart ached to *know* far beyond any belief or reasoning I might have gathered along my spiritual path. After what seemed a lifetime of yearning for spiritual truth—searching, seeking, and many years of deep prayer, meditation, and surrender—I pursued a career in spiritual study and became an ordained minister.

One day while sitting in my office I began to feel frustration over a project that simply wasn't coming together. I wasn't flowing, my efforts felt forced, and I was getting impatient. I decided to walk away from the endeavor and give myself a break, hoping to rekindle the flow by shifting my focus. This had always worked for me in the past.

I found myself walking on the beautiful grounds of the ministerial school where I was employed as a teacher, and eventually entered my favorite place—a small prayer chapel.

The chapel was empty. I sat down directly in front of a portrait of Christ, closed my eyes, and began to drink of the Niagara of peace that was always present in this sacred place.

Immediately I heard a Voice say very distinctly, *"You are here to help My children accept My Grace. Use The Book of Love."* Oh, my God! (Well, that is an understatement!) I opened my eyes to see if anyone was there. No one was present except I and the *Voice.* The Voice seemed to come from everywhere—inside, outside, above, below, beneath, behind, and most clearly, from within. *"You are here to help My children accept My Grace. Use The Book of Love."* I had been given my mission.

I was dumbfounded, totally humbled, in awe, overwhelmed, and blown away. "Glory bumps," as a friend of mine calls them, were running from head to toe. Then feelings of great despair engulfed me; I experienced myself plummeting back into earth awareness with incredible speed. I felt like I was falling from heaven, and my parachute wasn't going to open. Fear gripped me on all sides. It felt like an impossible mission beyond my capability to fulfill. I wasn't trained for the assignment nor was I well versed in the subject of Grace. I was afraid I would self destruct in five seconds, but, of course, I didn't.

My education as a minister on the subject of Grace had barely skimmed the surface of this seemingly mysterious phenomenon. How was I to help others understand Grace if I knew so little about it myself? My awareness of this benevolent mystery was limited to a very simplistic definition of it as 'a blessing from God that appeared out of nowhere and for no reason.' It was bestowed as an act of unexplainable intervention upon the deserving or the undeserving—God's choice! Surely, God didn't need my assistance.

All I could think of was perhaps my saving Grace would be revealed through the gospel I loved so much, *The Gospel According to John.* Had I not always identified that as *The Book of Love?* This I pondered as I rushed back to my office, but I had read *John* many times and didn't remember Jesus ever offering

teachings on the subject of my assignment. I would read it
again—and again, and thrice over. Jesus never used the word, or
at least it was never recorded.

Grace was, however, referenced in the first chapter of *John*
by the author. I decided to write out each sentence that contained
the word Grace and meditate upon the sentence:

> *"And the Word (Jesus Christ) became flesh and dwelt among us, full*
> *of grace and truth ... And from his fullness have we all received, grace*
> *upon grace. For the law was given through Moses; grace and truth came*
> *through Jesus Christ."*   *John 1: 14, 16-17 RSV*

Oh, my goodness—the Open Sesame to the hidden treasure
of Grace rested right before my eyes! How many times had I
read those words and never made the connection? Grace was
not just a random bestowing of love from God; it was much,
much more. It was the *consciousness*, the *awareness of the mind
of Christ Jesus* expressing in its fullness, and these inspired
words from the author of *John* were acknowledging that same
consciousness in us. We "***have***" all received it! It is a given!

When I added a few more passages to the ones surrounding
the word 'Grace,' the window of understanding became even
more expansive:

> *"The true light that enlightens every man was coming into the*
> *world ... In the beginning (this light) was the Word, and the Word was*
> *with God, and the Word was God. ...And the Word became flesh and*
> *dwelt among us full of grace and truth; ... And from his fullness have*
> *we all received, grace upon grace. For the law was given through (the*
> *consciousness of) Moses; grace and truth came through (the consciousness*
> *of) Jesus Christ."*   *John 1:9, 1, 14, 16 - 17 RSV*

The "light" referenced in this passage is a synonym for
the "Word," a visual of great magnitude. The "Word" is the
Divine idea for humankind encoded in the seed of every soul.
This Word is the image and likeness of God, the offspring of

the Divine expressing as "the true light that enlightens every man," woman and child as their individualized God Mind or Gracemind consciousness.

The fulfillment of this seed was exemplified in its perfection in Jesus Christ, the Word made flesh. This Word was "full of grace and truth." The metaphysical meaning of the word "truth," in relationship to "grace" in this scripture acknowledges the *laws* of consciousness functioning true to the nature of Gracemind that empowered Jesus to perform miracles. Later in the scriptures, Jesus said he didn't come to abolish the *law* (the truth) but to fulfill it. And, so he did from the consciousness of Gracemind true to his Divine nature, the Word made flesh.

Jesus is never recorded in the Gospels as having used the word 'Grace,' because the people of his time had no previous reference or teachings of it. They were entrenched in Levitical Law, commandments—the 'thou shalt' and 'thou shalt not.' Metaphysically, Moses, in his fullness/consciousness, gave the people an understanding of the repercussions or blessings that would inevitably result as an effect of either disobedience or adherence to the laws of God. These teachings were grounded in the spiritual law of equal measure—eye for an eye, and tooth for a tooth. You disobey or keep the laws of God, and God is either gonna get ya or reward ya. These teachings, however, were not representative of the 'fulfillment of the law' which promises a return far surpassing equal measure *when activated from the true nature of Being, Gracemind awareness!* The returns from Gracemind are immeasurable gifts which mirror Divinity and all that is reflective of the kingdom of God. Jesus' consciousness ushered in this truth and claimed it as the truth for all of us. He would have to teach the principles of the consciousness of Gracemind through *the living of his life* and gift his awareness to us by calling it forth from his *Essence.* And so will we; thus, his reason for the invitation to *"Follow me."* (John 1:43)

Christ came to show us that we, too, in our awakened state, are this living Word, this Light of God, expressing as the way, the truth, and the life. His journey on Earth, his life, teachings, and miracles show us the majesty, mystery, and multiplicity of the expression of this Word living life fully and completely in harmony with the Divine nature of the human Spirit.

Grace is the 'state of consciousness' from which Jesus functioned in the world. It was his awareness of himself as the living Word of God, image and likeness of his Father, inheritor of the kingdom, Gracemind, and the All therein. Not only that, these words clearly confirm that same truth for you—me, us, we, all! *"The true light that enlightens every man was coming into the world. ... And from his fullness, have we all received, grace upon grace." (John 1:9, 16)*

What I have written, up to this point, barely scratches the surface of describing the *Essence* of Gracemind and how it functions in us. It is important for us to recognize what has been revealed is the foundation that has been poured which will support future building blocks in consciousness for our high-rise to stand upon. Therefore, be ye not surprised to find expanding depths of meaning to these words of Grace and truth in future chapters of this book. The nature of Grace always deals with expansion, more. The meaning of Grace cannot be boxed or solidified in the mind. By the nature of Grace itself, our minds will be scattered, emptied, and refilled many times before our final emergence.

Being gifted with eyes to see the inner meaning of the first chapter of *John* was my first miracle. I felt like Steve Martin in 'LA Story' watching the words upon the neon sign before him change into a personal message from heaven, and I wanted to hug the words from *John* that now appeared as my personal message. These words would guide my way into an incredible journey of 'uncovery' as I studied the consciousness expressing through Jesus' ministry of unconditional love. My journey would unmask a bushel of *content* (mental baggage) that was not true to the *Essence* of my own Being. It would take me into the exploration of pastures of consciousness I never dreamed existed within my soul. Eventually, I would be enfolded in the arms of Grace as a realized state of Mind from which I now offer assistance to those who have ears to hear. Are you ready to hear? Regardless, this message of Grace will reach you, for it is the Voice without a voice that echoes in the silent chambers of *your* heart. Gracemind is simply your Sleeping Beauty awaiting the kiss of the Beloved, so that you might awaken from a drugged sleep and live happily ever after.

Come, Beloved, let's walk side by side as we explore even deeper levels of the awakening processes that accompany this miraculous transformation of soul. It is truly a Grace-full journey when seen through the eyes of our indwelling Christ Spirit, the Word made flesh. I promise you, your yearnings will be fulfilled by the fulfillment that already rests in you.

The Story of Your Yearning

To understand the nature of yearning is the first step in the journey of *Grace Awakening Essence.* The seed of yearning is the whisper of Spirit at the center of itself in you to know, to be, and to live in full awareness of the Essence of your Being. It is the call of the Divine, the All of individualized God expression as you, to accept the fulfillment of the Book of Life written in your heart. This yearning is experienced as your heart desires for good, love, peace and harmony; for joy, abundance, creativity and outlets of expression; for friendships and love relationships. It is experienced as the passion for freedom and the compulsion toward forgiveness. Triumph, overcoming challenges, success, all of these are yearning impulses from your true nature—the Essence of your Being or what I call *Gracemind.* And the beauty of it is, all of the above yearnings are fulfilled when the answer to the question 'who am I' is revealed. This is probably the most intense yearning in your heart right now, or you would not be reading this book.

'Who am I?' is the ultimate question—the most important question of all life. I promise you, the answer to this question sets you free in awareness, not only to be who you truly are, but to have all that is yours by Divine inheritance. The Greeks were aware that this contemplation was the purpose for our existence in this world. They left us with the eternal wisdom: "Know thyself!" So, what is your response to this question?

A few people, but not many, give an answer that reflects their name, vocation, or some title bestowed upon them as the result of their education, study, or current life choice. It is true we all have a name, and most of us identify ourselves with reference to our vocations or stations in life. For example, most people know me as one or more of the following: Diadra Price, wife, mother, ordained minister, prayer therapist, author, and public speaker. But, as we grow in truth, we take the 'who am I' question to deeper levels; we begin to reduce those qualifiers, or at least understand them as descriptions of the choices we have made in life that fit into a certain category or mold of expression—and expression only. They are simply labels that correspond to choices we have made. As we become more spiritually awake, we begin to see them as worldly titles with less and less importance or relevance to our true identity.

Because of an impulse from the Essence of your Being to *know* who you truly are, you will not rest until that knowing arrives upon the throne of awareness expressing in its fullness. None of the above-mentioned qualifiers satisfies the innate yearning to know, for they are not reflective of the fullest answer to the question. Your spiritual search always leads you inward, not outward, to draw you closer and closer to the eternal truth of your identity.

Because you are interested in spiritual growth, you may have answered the question with one of these responses: "I am a child of God, or I am the love of God, or I am the image and likeness of God." You may have even ventured to say, "I am God, or I am God in expression." Well, good for you, all of that is true, very true. However, I now ask you to contemplate something you may never have considered. Begin to identify yourself *as* the Grace of God, and in that truth do you live, move, and have eternal life. *You* are the Grace of God!

Until now, most of you have identified Grace as an effect or gift bestowed upon you as a miracle or spiritual blessing of some incredible good by God. You understand it to function something like intervention or undeserved blessings bestowed upon you without understanding the reason. You don't appear to have earned it by right of any action, belief, or beseeching prayer. You can't seem to make Grace fit into any linear theology that responds to reason, logic, or even the law of cause and effect (which more accurately should be termed 'the law of cause AS effect) related to the creative process. (We will explore the creative process in a later chapter.) There is some truth in this understanding of Grace, but it is far from the depth of truth that seeks to be made known.

You may never know how Grace functions or even why, but you are destined to realize *that* it functions through you *as you*. You are the gift of Grace, you are the miracle of Grace, and that Grace is seeking to function through you as the outpouring of infinite good, infinite blessings, and infinite miracles *all the time*. This aspect of the true nature of your Being is far beyond what the reasoning mind is able to comprehend. You, as Grace, can only be known and experienced by the livingness of it—just as it was for Jesus.

As this Essence beckons you, your first impulse is perceived through the streetcar named 'Desire.' Eastern philosophy would point to the pitfalls of desire and have you set a goal for its elimination. That is not possible, for desire is a built-in component of consciousness that functions much like the sunlight drawing forth new expression in the earth. While desire can become twisted and used as a tactic of the ego for selfish gain, this does not negate the truth that desire is an eternal spiritual impulse—a tapping at the door of awareness seeking admission and receptivity. It is experienced as a yearning for good.

There is a passage from a book that was extremely influential in my early states of the awakening spiritual journey. The more I took it to heart, the more truth it revealed. I offer it to you here as confirmation of the Source of your yearning. As the 'I' of you scans these words from the Voice of the Cosmic Christ, may they awaken in you an acceptance of your heart's desires at the level of their fulfillment. May they also bring you into a more expanded awareness of the true purpose of desire.

"Ask yourself, if you will, what is desire and why do I give it to you? Can you not see? It is My sign to you that I propose giving you or 'out-manifesting' for you that which already exists within you in Spirit, or in My Mind, and of which the desire is but the reflection, aye, it is My promise of so doing.

Think, could it be otherwise? Could a desire be, if its fulfillment were not already accomplished in My Mind? What possible other purpose could I have in permitting your mind to see it, if not to bring it forth? And if I thus make you aware of My purpose, it is but to prepare your mind so that it will co-operate with Me in the bringing of it forth.

For desire and its accomplishment are one and the same. Every desire, once born in the heart, is already fulfilled in actuality—that is, in My Mind, and but awaits your acceptance of it to come forth into manifestation.

One who knows this, instead of longing for and seeking and straining by mental and material means to bring it about for personal use, merely calls it to him, accepts it and possesses it, and in loving appreciation thanks God for being permitted to use it and to assist Him in His Purpose.

Know My child, that this is a simple law, but how hard and difficult you have made it for it to work for you and for your good!"

Reprinted from THE WAY TO THE KINGDOM by Anonymous | pp. 154-155 | DeVorss Publications 1932 | 0875161642 | www.devorss.com

This beautiful passage dawns a new light upon your eternal yearning. The understanding found here shifts the meaning of desire from being a yearning for something you do not have, to being an impulse of God's Will to entice you to *accept* what is *already* fulfilled. It aligns your conscious mind appropriately to its rightful position of receptivity, acceptance, and trust. It heals the pains of doubt and confusion that accompany any sense of separation. It changes the direction of your mind from looking to the world for fulfillment and positions your soul into its inherited posture of receivership from Source. Whatever you desire is already yours in God Mind. Your desires are the reflections of promises kept in the heart of God Mind at the center of your Being which are simply awaiting your full acceptance.

The manifestations of your deep desires are not dependant upon your beliefs, affirmations, or longings, but on the Essence within the ideas they represent. I use the analogy of the seed, as did Christ, to illustrate. The seed is *unable* to reflect back upon itself and question the impulse of its nature to become that which is its destiny. It simply totally accepts, allows, and rests within itself as its God Essence manifests the image and likeness of the Divine selection (or Divine idea) known as apple tree or rose, bearing fruit or blossom. You, however, with your expanded degree of awareness, have the capacity to reflect upon the idea or seed desire. If reflection is in harmony with the manifesting principles of abundance, acceptance, and freedom (we will discuss these principles of the laws of Grace in the next chapter), the Essence within the seed evolves itself into manifestation reflecting the perfection of the Divine idea contained within its original design.

Reflection within the mind is capable of (what appear to be) only two movements—acceptance or rejection. You will see later how these two movements are in actuality one movement of acceptance. Doubt, despair, and regret express as choices of rejection and become the *accepted* environment in which the seed cannot flourish. I firmly believe these energies of mind are impulsed by the failure to understand the relationship between the seed, the sower of the seed, the one reflecting upon the seed, and the fulfillment within the seed. These are, in the Absolute, ONE! If rejected as the result of negative thoughts and feelings, the desire is either repressed, depressed, or—at worst—aborts or dies until the Farmer (God Mind) sows again—which may or may not be in this lifetime. If your desires are not fulfilled, it is because doubt, despair, regret, indecision, or rejection has emerged as the choice accepted from a sense of separation.

Desire is an inherent movement within consciousness, involving and evolving Divine ideas through the creative process. It is a continuous flow of infinite possibilities surfacing from Gracemind to your conscious mind. Ideas received as pure desires are images that represent what is written in your heart that are seeking to be made manifest. Desire is the communicative mechanism of God seeking acceptance at the level of spiritual expression.

In some of my classes the question often arises as to how specific you should be as you move into prayer with desire. Do you architect your desires so that you are explicit about what you want, or do you surrender the details and specifics to God, knowing God knows how, when, and what is best for you? This type of question arises only in the mind of one who is experiencing a sense of separation from God. The question is not relevant in Grace consciousness. One living from Grace KNOWS ALL DESIRE IS OF THE INDWELLING FATHER and *carries its fulfillment as an inevitable manifestation.* The idea within the desire is already fulfilled within itself and simply awaits a fertile soil in consciousness to receive it. As I have vehemently expressed, fulfillment rests within the seed of the desire, independent of the specifics you may bring into prayer.

Gracemind sees specificity as simply the activity of saying 'yes' to whatever pure desire is rising in the heart. As you become more attuned to the desire, you may be given greater detail about the form that desire will take. Whatever specifics are given from your God Mind to your inner vision, accept. You do not dictate specifics to God, the Originator of the desire. How egotistical can you get? The specifics are contained within the idea presented, resting in perfection and known to the Source, God I Am. You simply say "yes" with excitement and enthusiasm, absent attachment to outcome and income, and the need to know the specifics of how, when, where, and what. If God Mind deems it important for your conscious mind to know greater details, they will be revealed. Otherwise, none of the above is any of your conscious business, for it creates unnecessary busyness at that level of your mind which may *enter-fear* with the unfolding of the perfect seed.

As you move through the following chapters you will see how all desire advances to the ultimate desire to know who you truly are, and how the fulfillment of that desire shifts your definition of desire from being a yearning for what you do not have, to being the acceptance of what is already yours. Such is the enlightenment from *Grace Awakening Essence.*

Chapter Two

The Gracing

Chapter 2

The Gracing

What we need to focus on now is *what* is the Essence of Grace consciousness and *how* does it function? In order to do that, I will present some new perceptions of words you have become familiar with in your spiritual studies.

Let's first of all look at the word *Mind* as the totality of your Divine inheritance. Created in the image and likeness of God, the Mind that is of God is the same Mind that is yours. I am not using the word 'Mind' with any correlation or relationship to your brain mind. Your brain mind is an organism of function. Your God Mind is ineffable, beyond anything that can be perceived, described, or even experienced.

The closest description that words can convey as a definition of Mind is that *Mind is All, and All is Mind.* Nothing exists *outside*, and all exists *as* Mind by its own definition. In the Aramaic, the original language of Jesus, the word *miltha* means 'word' which translates in meaning as 'energy of Mind.' *"In the beginning was the word ('energy of Mind')... And the Word ('energy of Mind') became flesh ..."* (John 1:1,14). That living Word has become flesh in us as it did in Jesus. It is the Essence of our Being, the same Mind energy.

Dr. Rocco Errico, one of the most renowned Bible scholars of our times, gives us deep insight as he helps us understand the original meaning of 'Word' from the Aramaic text.

"The Aramaic word 'miltha' simply and basically means 'the creative, prophetic, spoken word of God.' In the hymn-prologue of John's gospel, the 'Word becomes flesh,' i.e., it humanizes in and as the person of Jesus of Nazareth. According to John, the Word has a specific relationship with God. In other words, whatever God was, the Word was also—'In the beginning was the word, and that very word was with God and God was that very word.'

*The 'Word' is God as creative power. Divine Mind creates
through spiritual law. It is interesting to note that 'miltha' also
means 'energy of mind.' Thus, we may translate John 1:1 as
'In the beginning was energy of mind and that very energy of
mind was with God and God was that very energy of mind.' The
'Word' and the divine movement of creating are the same."*

Science of Mind Magazine, Article titled "Light From the
Language of Jesus," August 1992, by Dr. Rocco Errico, Ph.D.,
Th.D.

Life is the movement of Mind energy in creation—mass
producing, imaging the likeness of itself, molding, reflecting,
mirroring All in all. As the All, Mind is Omnipresence (all
presence), Omnipotence (all power), and Omniscience (all
knowingness). It is the Essence out of which all things come into
being. It is all life, energy, light, universal ethers, cosmic design,
worlds within worlds, universes, formlessness, and form.

There are three basic components of Mind energy that
I reference as our spiritual DNA (Divine Nature Attributes)
inheritance. They are Peace, Love, and Joy. When referencing
Peace, Love, and Joy as your spiritual DNA, I will capitalize
these words in this text. As I define these components from
Gracemind awareness, you must be willing to lay down your
current contextual definitions and carry these forward. Your
definitions of peace, love, and joy are derived from your
brain mind which has observed peace, love, and joy through
comparables of opposites. You understand peace in relationship
to its seeming opposite, chaos. Love is perceived as either
conditional or unconditional, and joy is your experience when
everything in this world is not in opposition to your expectations.
As your eyes scan these new definitions, feel your mind opening,
expanding, and accepting your Divine inheritance at a level of
wisdom that before has been sealed until you were ready. You
are ready now, or this book would not be resting in your hands.

Peace is the sphere of pure consciousness wherein all ideas rest in their fulfillment, yet to describe it as a sphere or as pure consciousness is misleading. For there to be a 'sphere,' you can only perceive it as a place you can go or something you can experience. Peace is not a place, nor is it an experience—it is all place in a sea of no place that contains the All. Pure consciousness, as part of this definition, though not measurable, is at least accessible to our awareness by the experience of focus. But you must not try to grab hold of your Divine inheritance of Peace by understanding any definition. Let Peace embrace *you* from its internal, eternal beingness of what you already are. Just be aware that when you are *peaceful*, quiet, and still, the portal of your mind opens to more of your spiritual DNA. From the sphere of pure Peace all ideas and possibilities rise. From that same dimension they are already fulfilled.

As logic, content, belief, perception, and other mental activities become stilled or, better yet, absent from brain mind, the Mind of Peace, as a component of your spiritual DNA, consumes all unlike itself and remembers itself as Gracemind— the same Mind energy or consciousness that expressed in Jesus. Herein lies your salvation, your transformation, and your realized state of Grace. As I take you deeper into the exploration of the sea of consciousness, I will expand this definition of Peace. But for now, just let this definition begin to integrate into your mind.

Love is the *movement* of infinite Mind upon all the Divine ideas that rests in Peace. Love functions as Grace, the fulfillment of the law, by drawing into manifestation all these ideas in their original design. You can interchange the words 'Love' and 'Grace.' They are synonymous. Love is also synonymous with God's Will, being that it is the *moving force* that draws Divine ideas into manifestation if there is nothing to resist them. When your mind is functioning in Love, Gracemind is in place as the catalyst for the Will of God to manifest.

The Holy Spirit is the agent of Love. It is the movement of Mind energy that attracts the invisible into the visible by some impulse of Grace we may never understand. We don't

know 'how' it attracts or moves; we just know 'that' it does. In
its stirrings we can feel it, accept it, testify to it, but it can't be
captured, measured, or proved by any means of this world. Love
is the way and the means to the fulfillment of your dreams and
heart's desires, for it is the natural movement upon that which is
already fulfilled in the invisible, drawing it forth into the visible.

    You activate this benevolent movement through faith
and trust, total peace, and fearlessness of heart. You feel it as
stillness in the soul, even in a world of turmoil and chaos. Love
moves and gathers, it sows and reaps, it protects and embraces.
Love reveals and heals, it enlightens and teaches. Love draws
forth its own and transforms all into its image and likeness. Love
gifts the world with endless provisions. It calls forth the truth
and sets you free. Love brings to mind, from Mind itself, all
ideas to serve God's world. Love is the Gracemind that extends
itself through you and me to accept and embrace itself in all.

    Joy is the synthesis of Peace and Love as a state of
Mind energy experienced as happiness for *no reason*. Joy is
the inevitable outpouring of the energy of Mind as the matrix
of Gracemind consciousness. All enlightened Beings live,
move, and experience their Essence as a reservoir of Joy. It is
the eternal flow of the fountain of the living waters of spiritual
awareness. The Joy I speak of here is soft; it is neither high nor
low; it doesn't come and go, nor does it vacillate. It has no object
and needs no reason in order to be present. All Joy ever seeks
is empty space in mind to fill. It is a steady stream from the
eternal Source of eternal life. It is the natural state of Gracemind
impulsed from Peace and Love united.

    These three components—Peace, Love, and Joy—are the
Essence of your Divine inheritance. They are the spiritual DNA
of Gracemind that regenerate, transform, and evolve you into
the awareness of your original and eternal design. They are the
components of consciousness that make all things new. They are
your only truth, regardless of the content of your mind that may
tell you otherwise. They are forever echoing through your heart's
desires to be accepted. They are the magic and mystery that give

you birth, grow you into adulthood, and regenerate you life into
life. They are the eternal Essence of your spiritual citizenship
that promises you freedom. They are your God to love with
all your heart, all your soul, and all your mind. They are your
neighbor as your Self. They are your Jesus, your Christ, your
God Self. They are God's kingdom come, your heaven in sweet
Earth and beyond. They are you—the Essence of the God you
seek as your eternal life!

Principles of Grace in the Creative Process

There is a Reality that is ever constant, ever true, and
forever the same, always and in all ways, regardless of any
belief system or perceptions you may have gathered within your
experience of Reality. This eternal Reality is your saving Grace.

Teachings based in the nature of Reality have emerged
in every major religious movement. Movements that have
not incorporated these teachings have fallen to the wayside
and disappeared. Movements that have expanded have been
sustained by the nature of Reality at the core of their theology.
Of the seven major religions of the world, each one began with
wisdom teachings realized through a Being of great Light. In
the original texts of these religions can be found the same truth
expressed in myriad ways. If you do not believe this, I invite you
to take a few courses on comparative religion.

In my own search, I have been exposed to a multitude
of teachings, all of which contained seeds of the nature of
Reality, unveiling mysteries, buried treasures, and pearls of
great wisdom. I am indebted to all of them. Each has helped me
understand the nature of Reality and the nature of the spiritual
laws inherent within Reality. I think it is important to honor
and appreciate every step of your spiritual journey. It has been
a wonderful filtering and sorting process that has enriched your
soul. It has brought you up to this eternal moment of wisdom.

We are about to examine the spiritual laws that are embedded within the soul's code as components of consciousness involved in the *functioning* of the DNA of the nature of Being. These laws are eternal and true; they do not change, but the activity of these laws affect all change. They function as immutable principles of creation, as Mind energy in action, and you are that Mind energy, God Mind, image, and likeness of Peace, Love, and Joy. To be ignorant of these laws does not excuse you from their workings. Ignorance throws you into confusion, doubt, worry, and many other degenerative thought patterns. These thought patterns can become your predominant vibrational energetic focus. As such, they become content of mind, functioning as choice-makers that out-picture according to spiritual law.

The spiritual laws I am about to present are inherent within all major religions of the world. They are woven into various teachings and parables and have been acknowledged by a variety of different names. Simply stated these laws are the 'truth' that sets you free, reflective of the second word in the promise of your Divine inheritance of "grace and truth." These laws function within your spiritual DNA of Peace, Love and Joy. They are the agents of the creative process. By creative process, I mean the laws of Mind energy that function in the manifestation of form and experience. When totally understood and practiced from the awareness of Gracemind, they move within consciousness as principles or laws of governance in relationship to the experience of life as it was originally designed. They become the mystery solved and the answer to the questions of the soul as to *how* and *why* things are as they are. When there is alignment or complete cooperation with them, they bring into manifestation what is written in your heart. This is what is referred scripturally as the fulfillment of all the laws and the prophets.

The three components of your spiritual DNA—Peace, Love, and Joy—function as ***abundance, acceptance, and freedom.*** Awareness of these three principles and how they operate will expand your understanding of the definition of Grace as the fulfillment of the law. Christ said, from his consciousness of

Grace, *"Think not that I have come to abolish the law and the prophets; I have come not to abolish them, but to fulfill them."* (Matt. 5:17) These three spiritual laws can be understood more accurately as principles in the context of absoluteness, for they are forever eternal and true to their nature. They are the principles of consciousness as the matrix of the creative process, and by their nature they serve the soul of Essence.

Abundance is the first principle of Grace. God always functions in creation as abundance. Always! Consciousness always attracts more, never less. *Less does not exist as a creative principle within consciousness.* Those who have been sitting in New Thought circles for many years will recognize this principle as the law of cause and effect. This law has become the cliché, *thoughts held in mind produce after their kind.* This interpretation is not entirely correct because it lacks recognition of the component of Grace that always deals with increase. *Thoughts held in mind produce after their kind* implies an equal measure of return—or even-exchange—for the focus of concentration, input for output. However, Grace is the spiritual law of abundance that always guarantees *more* return than the measure that is given. *God always deals with increase, more. Less is not a part of God's laws.* Wherever and whatever is the focus of your mind will always bring unto you MORE—never less! THUS, if you focus on doubt, fear, resentment, lack, or being the victim, for example, you will attract MORE, an increase of those things in consciousness and experience. If you focus on plenty, health, or love in relationships, you will have MORE of those as your effect. It is important to note here that feelings are focus at an energetic level.

When Gracemind sits upon the throne of your awareness, the movement of that Mind is always reflective of the nature of God. From this position, the law is fulfilled and brings unto you an abundance of Peace, Love and Joy. Jesus knew his true nature to be a hologram of God's true nature of the abundance of Peace, Love, and Joy. Every activity of mind and heart was spawned

in him from this Essence, and it was sown abundantly. In his
earthly expression, Jesus never did anything contradictory to any
of these components. From this Essence he was empowered to
perform his abundant miracles, which always reflected the true
nature of life expressing its original design.

All of nature is true to this principle because there is
nothing in nature to resist it. Nature gives from the nature
of itself. A tomato gives its seeds unto the ground. It can't
help it. The ground accepts the seed and becomes a receptive
environment for the seed to grow. A tomato plant emerges, true
to the Essence within the seed. The tomato plant produces an
undetermined number of tomatoes with a multitude of seeds that,
in turn, give of themselves again, increasing exponentially in
number of fruit and seeds. It is endless, measureless, and always
more than can be accounted for. There is a spiritual message
of Grace expressed in the phrase, "*you can count the seeds in a
tomato, but you can't count the tomatoes in a seed.*" Such is the
nature of Grace functioning through the law of abundance.

Jesus knew his Divine nature to be the same as God's in
that God never deals in even-exchange. In order to fulfill the
law of Grace from his Divine nature, Jesus always expressed
himself in thought, word, and deed with no expectations or
need for an equal return. Realization that the law of abundance,
by its nature, cannot deal in even-exchange, opens a whole
new pasture for exploration in consciousness. If you desire to
experience Grace as the fulfillment of the law, you must ask
yourself where and how you insist on even-exchange, and then
drop that intention. At the end of this chapter, we will explore
that question in greater depth.

Expanded awareness of this principle offers a more in-depth
definition of Grace:

*Grace is the nature of the spiritual law of abundance that
does not deal in even-exchange but with the increase of the
expression of the true nature of your Being. In this expression,
the law is fulfilled.*

This understanding of the law of Grace consciousness makes the definition of Grace as 'the fulfillment of the law' more clear. Grace, as the fulfillment of the law of consciousness is directly proportional to the expression of your thoughts, feelings, and actions aligned with your spiritual DNA—not the content of your mind.

The good news is, if there is any perception or content of mind that is not aligned with your true nature, by Grace this can be rectified. Grace always self-corrects if it is allowed. Grace redeems the soul and saves it from the constant merry-go-round of karmic law which appears to deal in even-exchange. Grace is the power within you to overcome and transform any negative state of consciousness or outer manifestation. It heals, purifies, regenerates, and restores you to your natural state of wholeness—effortlessly. You will have an opportunity to look at your part in this redemption as you answer the questions at the end of this chapter. For now, let's explore the second principle of Grace—acceptance.

Acceptance is the nature of consciousness within original design that is forever giving and receiving from itself, to itself, as itself. It is your nature to accept, and to accept all. God is All, and all is God. The nature of God always accepts itself. It cannot do otherwise, and you are the microcosm of the macrocosmic God. Until the all of you rests in total acceptance on every level of awareness, Gracemind cannot sit upon the throne of consciousness to make all things new in alignment with original design, and the law cannot be fulfilled.

Once again you can look to nature for this Reality of truth. All of nature accepts itself. It does not resist any aspect of its own nature—not in form, not in growth, and not in purpose or expression. Nature always accepts the totality of all there is. All of itself is accepted, and there is no conflict or resistance to any other expression of God. The tree rests within itself in perfect Peace. It does not resist its own nature. It accepts what it has to offer to the world and what the world has to offer to it. It gifts both the meditating Buddha and the thief with total acceptance as they rest beneath its branches. This is unconditional acceptance at a very deep level of the true nature of original design.

There are four essential levels of acceptance that are operative in the consciousness of humanity. The first is *acceptance at the level of self,* which automatically includes others because of the oneness factor. Can you unequivocally accept yourself 'as is'? Can you accept your body and the content of your mind? Can you accept your spirituality and your humanness? Can you accept the seeming flaws in your perfection? That's an oxymoron, to be sure. How about your past, present, and future as your eternal always? What about your situations and your circumstances? Can you accept all of you and, therefore, all of me? If your answer is '*no*' to any of these, ironically it is '*yes*' to what you seemingly can't accept. The nature of this principle is designed to only accept. *No* as a resistance factor is not an option in the Reality of consciousness, for a '*no*' from your mortal mind is always a '*yes*' from your Gracemind. Let me explain. *The nature of Gracemind can only accept;* this is an eternal principle or law of consciousness. You have *accepted what you resist* when you seemingly can't accept. That position of resistance becomes a focused magnetic attraction for *more* of what you attempt to reject. Thus, you have accepted the unacceptable.

At the core of any resistance are the elements of judgment and fear, and consciousness does not distinguish the choices of judgment and fear from any other choice. All expression is accepted at the vibrational level of the Mind energy that is expressed. According to the law, an attempt to reject or not accept from a thought or feeling of judgment or fear will always multiply more of what you don't want.

The only way consciousness can say 'no' to something is by making an alternative choice of what is desired. For example: you can say 'no' to sugar as a simple choice by choosing a sugar substitute or no sugar at all. In this action you accept sugar for what it is, absent of any judgment on your part. However, if you judge sugar as bad or unhealthy, your judgment becomes the accepted energy of Mind, that, by its nature of acceptance, multiplies a return true to the perception or evaluation that surrounds sugar. Your resistance to sugar will then show up as temptation—everywhere, and it will increase the possibility of an unhealthy reaction from your body. Resistance, in the form of unacceptability, perpetuates what is resisted because of this law and the law of abundance. Yes, make your choices for 'no,' but make them through alternative choices and without judgment. This helps you understand the great truth revealed in the simple statement, "What you resist persists."

As you study the laws of Reality, it is important to remember none of these laws contain opposites; each is non-dual in nature. Abundance does not contain lack, Acceptance does not contain rejection, and Freedom does not contain confinement. Each law functions perfectly for all individuals and is true to its original design. Like electricity, each is impersonally personal to the user. You will find this to be true in all three of these cosmic principles of creation.

The second level of acceptance is the *level of receiving.* Can you receive without the need to give in return? If you immediately feel the need to give in return, you have fallen into even-exchange consciousness, which keeps you bound under karma (in experience only), instead of living freely from the consciousness of Grace. Can you receive without the need to have earned the gift? Again, you are facing the same dilemma if you cannot freely accept what is given. The law of acceptance within Gracemind always receives unconditionally.

Resistance to receiving presents itself as guilt, unworthiness, judgment, fear, shame, and the need to earn. If you look deeply into the mirror of your soul and find any of these resistors, recognize them as your greatest possessions, and offer them up as your gift of love to Grace. Grace transforms all into the image and likeness of itself and eagerly awaits your offering. What greater gift could you offer than your seemingly greatest possessions?

The third level of acceptance is the *level of giving.* Giving is your true nature, and each person is compelled by his/her Divinity to profusely express this quality of soul. The slightest degree of withholding or conditional giving aborts the true expression of your nature and results in a miscarriage of the life that is seeking to expand through you in the giving process. I suggest you make a list of the myriad acts of giving you engage in each day in order to recognize the motives, intentions, and arenas of life where you participate. You will be amazed at what you uncover.

When you look with Gracemind into giving, you will see a deeper aspect of receiving. Anything given, whether it is a thought, feeling, or action, is first received by you. When giving is understood as 'receiving *and* being true to your nature,' and this understanding is applied in every aspect of living, then Gracemind is in place. Your world experience then mirrors the kingdom of heaven that dwells within you—the miracles of Grace.

It is your nature to give, and from that nature you receive and accept. Again, let me explain. I was once in meditation in the act of forgiveness—giving up a long held resentment for a seemingly unjustified act. As I brought the person associated with this act to my awareness, offering forgiveness, my inner vision was engulfed with a picture of a skeleton. The inner Voice interpreted, "**It registers in your bones first.**" That experience left me with an unprecedented new awareness of the nature of giving. Whatever is given registers in our bones first, be it a thought, feeling, or action. We receive first, then the one to whom we are giving receives as well. In addition, because of the *Oneness* of the All of creation, all receives. From this awareness, the old saying, "the gift is in the giving," takes on new meaning.

There was a true story reported in the April 1985 issue of *Guidepost Magazine* that was one of the most inspirational, moving, miraculous examples of the power of Grace consciousness affecting the healing of a dear soul named Barbara Cummiskey. This story made my message of "it registers in your bones first" come alive with spiritual understanding. A portion of that article is reprinted here with permission from *Guideposts Magazine*:

In 1965, I'd been a typical, active 15-year old who loved gymnastics, played the flute in the high school orchestra, worked at an after-school job and headed the youth group at my church. My mother said she hadn't seen me sit still for 10 minutes in three years.

But then weird things started happening. One day in gym class I couldn't get my left hand to grasp the flying rings. That night, I slipped on the stairs at home, and I slipped again the next day at school. "Just part of growing up," the doctor said. "Your symptoms will disappear in time." But they didn't.

So I lurched down hallways, every step taking me farther into the unknown. After a while came double vision, then a brace for a left arm that was turning more and more into itself. I underwent one test after another, but nothing led to a diagnosis. I started college but had to drop out; I just wasn't well enough. More tests. More symptoms. More problems.

*Finally, in 1970, my doctor had some concrete information for me. "We've identified your condition, Barbara," he said. "You have **MS**—multiple sclerosis. It usually doesn't strike people quite so young as yourself."*

"What do we do now?" I asked.

My doctor shook his head. "I'll tell you the truth, there's almost nothing we can do. This disease is slowly going to short-circuit your central nervous system because it hardens the tissue around your brain and spine. The wrong messages go to various parts of your body and they don't function as they should. The severity varies. We can only hope your case is a mild one."

*Very soon, the course my **MS** was taking became clear. Twice, in 1971 and 1972, my heart and lungs failed, and I was rushed to the hospital, near death. Then there was a period of stability when I neither got better nor very much worse—a common occurrence in MS. I attended college as a handicapped student and later worked as a secretary. But the virulence of the disease was merely interrupted. I went from a cane to crutches. Inside my body, vital organs were beginning to fail. A partly paralyzed diaphragm made breathing difficult and asthma and pneumonia became chronic problems. I needed a Foley* *catheter for bladder control and, when I lost bowel function, an ileostomy.*

By 1978, I was in a wheelchair—my feet and hands curled and all but useless—and I required a constant supply of oxygen. That year, I went to the Mayo Clinic, hoping to discover new techniques to help my labored breathing. There weren't any. Clinic doctors didn't hold out false hope. "Pray, Barbara," they told me. "Nothing we can do will stop the deterioration."

... Over the next few years my church pastor, Meredith Bailie, became a special friend, visiting me day after day in the hospital and when I was bedridden at home.

It was Pastor Bailie who helped me discover what I needed most: a goal, one even a disabled person could strive for. And the goal was to grow in faith. It became my "job," something I could do despite all the pain and loss of bodily capacity, and I worked at it.

... Now, after the grim visit to Mayo, I felt a new urgency about my connection to God. The less physical health I had, the more I yearned for spiritual health.

I cried out to God. "Please! Please! I can't even read Your word anymore. I need something to do."

Over and over I pleaded for something to counteract the fact that I could barely move. I craved activity. Action. I called out to God for it.

His answer came. Not in a flash, not overnight, but through prayer itself: Praying is action. Pray for others.

How simple. How possible! Until that thought came to me, I had seen prayer as passive. Now I saw that praying for others could be my gymnastics, my flute-playing, my special activity.

I had prayed for others before, but now it became a compelling need, a vocation. I spent hours in prayer ... . When friends came over, I would ask them to read to me or pray with me.

... My condition continued to worsen. A lung collapsed. Most of the time I could barely see; technically I was blind. In 1980, I had a tracheotomy—an incision was made in my windpipe to allow a more direct connection to my oxygen supply.

My parents had made changes in our house to accommodate my needs—for my electric wheelchair, a hospital bed for me and tubing running through three rooms so I could hook up to my oxygen concentrator in different locations. Everyone knew I was dying. My doctors confirmed it. My mother and father and I began counseling with the Hospice Volunteers ....

Then came June 7, 1981.

It was a Sunday, my sister Jan's 29th birthday. She was coming over to celebrate and I looked forward to giving my mother at least some token help with making the cake. I remember thinking what a bright clear birthday it was when my mother came into my room. "Ready to give the cake batter a few licks?" she asked. I nodded. With my mother helping, I began the struggle to hitch myself out of bed and into my wheelchair; my legs had begun drawing into a fetal position and it was impossible for me to put my feet flat on the floor. We transferred tubing on my tracheotomy to the oxygen supply mounted on my wheelchair, gathered my various receptacles around me and then I used my forearm to push down the starter lever on my wheelchair.

In the kitchen, I managed to stir the cake batter a couple of times despite the fact that my hands had turned inward to the point where my fingers almost touched my wrists. By now, even that small effort was enough to exhaust me and I asked my mother to help me get back into bed. She did, and went back to finish the cake for Jan's birthday.

*After a while, my Aunt Ruthie came to my room to read letters and cards from people who listened to a Chicago radio station ... . Most of the well-wishers mentioned that they were praying for me. My aunt left to help my mother and, shortly after noon, two friends, Joyce Jugan and Angela Crawford, popped in after the morning worship service at my church. Then, as the three of us visited, I heard a fourth **voice**. A firm, audible **voice** over my left shoulder.*

*"My child, get up and walk!" Startled, I looked at my friends. I could see that they had not heard the **voice**. But I was certain that I had heard it.*

"Joyce! Angela!" I blurted, *"God just spoke to me. He said to get up and walk. I heard Him."*

The two women stared at me.

"I know, I know, it's weird," I said. *"But God really did speak to me. Please, run and get my family. I want them!"*

They flew out to the hallway, called my sisters and parents and rushed back into the room. I couldn't wait any longer. I took the oxygen tube from my throat, removed the brace from my arm and actually jumped out of bed. And there I stood, on two legs that hadn't held the weight of my body in over five years.

This wasn't possible, of course—there were 1,001 medical reasons why this couldn't be happening. Yet here I stood, firmly, solidly, feeling tingly all over, as if I had just stepped from an invigorating shower. I could breathe freely. And I could see—I could see me. A whole, healthy me. My hands were normal, not curled to my wrists. The muscles in my arms and legs were filled out and whole. My feet were flat to the ground, like a dancer's. And oh, the step I danced as I headed toward the doorway. I met my mother in the hallway. She stopped short, and then she lifted the hem of my nightgown. Her eyes widened, her arms flung wide. "Barbara," she cried. "You have calves again!"

Dad was on the wheelchair ramp to the family room. Speechless, he wrapped me in his arms and waltzed me around and around. Then everyone—my parents, Aunt Ruthie, Jan, my teenage sister Amy—applauded wildly while I tried some ballet steps I hadn't done in 16 years. Next I walked to the couch, sat down—and stood up again. Down. Up. Down up. Six times in a row.

Angela Crawford, an occupational therapist, hardly knew what she was saying: "B-but, Barb, you can't ….." She took my pulse and exclaimed, "Barb, you've just wrecked everything I learned in school! You're absolutely normal; it's really a miracle!"

*… I don't know why God healed me. I don't believe I "earned" or "deserved" a healing any more than I "deserved" **MS**. I only know that on the morning of June 7, 1981, I felt good about myself—mentally, emotionally and spiritually well.*

Through my prayer life, I was a busy, active member of the human family—not running or jumping or even walking like most people, but not separated from them by bitterness, self-pity or despair. My mind and spirit were healthy and whole.
    And then God made my body whole, too.

Perhaps dear Barbara, the miracle-working power of God's Grace was activated through the law of attraction as you prayed in the consciousness of oneness with all and in the awareness of the Peace, Love, and Joy of God moving through those for whom you prayed. Perhaps dear Barbara, that Grace consciousness registered in your bones first, and over time, consumed the disease of your body—not to mention the good works your prayers accomplished as they registered in the bones of others. Perhaps dear Barbara, the Voice of God could be heard in you because of the purity of your mind and heart that opened a direct line of communication from your superconscious to your conscious. Praying for others is the highest expression of giving, for it not only is a gift to others but a gift unto your Self. Praise God!

The fourth level of acceptance is the *level of what is*. Can you accept what is in the world without the need to change or fix it? This is the real toughie; it presents the greatest challenge because of a deeply ingrained sense of right and wrong, or good versus evil. From the perception of a dualistic world, this will always be the tendency. This level of acceptance is not asking you to sanction any act, situation, or experience; it is simply asking you *not to judge it*. Judgment is not possible in Gracemind awareness, for here only Peace, Love, and Joy abide. Judgment is deemed a sin in every religion. Never forget that judgment *accepts* at the level of the error and multiplies the condition. Don't fall into judging another's judgment either, or you will be following another's error and reap the same harvest.

When doubt, fear, worry, and other negative states are present in a consciousness that is trying to realize abundance and acceptance, these focused energies are subject to the perfection of the principle and they become acceptably abundant. Then, you wonder why you experience what appears to be an opposite manifestation of your affirmations and prayers. Again, also remember, feeling is focus as content of consciousness and, therefore, subject to these principles as well. You cannot separate feelings from thoughts, for feelings are the children of thoughts and subject to the same principles in the creative process.

We are required to accept all at the level of what is. This is similar to going to a sale and buying something that has a sticker on it that says, "As Is." We can decide to take it home with us—as is, or leave it there—as is. It doesn't mean we won't be guided to repair it at another time, or remake it to suit our needs should we decide to keep it. It does mean we are first required to accept it AS IS! Nothing can change until what is expressing is first accepted. Again, to not accept As Is, is to accept what is not acceptable; as a result, the 'not acceptable' inevitably multiplies.

God's principles are perfect because they never deviate from their Essence. Much like the principle of mathematics, God's principles of consciousness are always true to function, regardless of the user's capacity to apply the principles with understanding. We can attempt to multiply one number by another according to the mathematical principle of multiplication, but unless we are true to the principle, we will emerge with an incorrect answer. The same is true for the principles of abundance and acceptance in the creative process.

Freedom is a principle of Grace functioning within the laws of Being. It is innate as a characteristic of the Divine idea for humankind and for the All. It must be understood as the core impulse of the Life Force which impels individual expression, evolution, and all creativity within the Divine Plan. It is inclusive of the concept of freewill, and when freedom or freewill is threatened, the soul of any life expression automatically resists. This explains our spontaneous resistance to anything or anyone who tries to control, confine, imprison, or limit us mentally, emotionally, or physically. Our response to freedom's threat is always from the fear of annihilation of this eternal aspect of our true nature. The truth is, *"Nothing real can be threatened, nothing unreal exists."* (A Course In Miracles, Introduction) And when we remember the truth that we are the 'Real' that cannot be threatened or annihilated, our resistance to a seeming threat to our freedom disappears. It is important to note: there is no 'free will,' as in a will separate from God, but there is forever *freewill* within the only Will of God functioning in the creative process as the eternal nature of freedom inherent to the All.

Freedom functions as an aspect of our Divinity; it compels us to choose and experience the consequences of our choices according to spiritual law. Freewill choices, aligned with spiritual DNA and the individual seed code of original design, are always impulsed from the Essence of Being. These choices produce effects reflective of all we are created to be and do. When our mind is not aligned with spiritual DNA, we make choices from a sense of separation. More often than not, this results in pain and suffering as the effect of an egoic sense of free will choice.

Important Note:

In this world, no matter what you choose, an alternative choice is always possible. Your freedom lies in your gift of freewill choice within an infinite possibility of seemingly opposite choices. However, because of the inner workings of the laws of abundance and acceptance, your freedom is limited to a choice of only 'yes.' If you truly understand this, would you not choose 'yes' to what is written in your heart, according to original design? Of course you would. Then surrender all, by offering freedom to all through your indwelling Spirit, and Spirit will choose through you, as you, and in perfect alignment with what is written in your heart.

These three principles of Grace are the energetics of consciousness at the center of your Being that comprise the components or matrix of the only true and eternal states of

Mind energy. They are your Divine inheritance at work in the creative process. They are the Essence of your Being. In and of themselves, they seek to be made flesh in you, as you, and as your life experience. They are spiritual laws of truth that are forever seeding/seeking to be fulfilled by/as the Grace you already are. These principles continually unfold your Essence and gift you with your experience of Reality. They are intrinsic within the nature of consciousness and perpetually operative in the creative process. Whether your experience is true to Reality or reflective of the illusions of mentalism will be determined by your ability to understand, accept, and apply these principles.

The Law Fulfilled

As I continued to look for the Grace teachings of Jesus in *The Book of Love,* I could see a stream of consciousness prevalent in many of his parables and words. He continually offered a way of living that was dramatically different from the norm of the times. The people had previously been taught that following the laws of God guaranteed a return of even-exchange; the measure of giving would equal the measure of return. Obedience to the law would bring an equal measure of approval from God, whereas sin would be met with an appropriate punishment. Jesus said he did not come to destroy the law but to fulfill it—what exactly did he mean by this? He meant the law functions according to an immutable principle of return, and when the law was applied from the true nature of Essence, our spiritual DNA of Peace, Love, and Joy, it would be returned in abundance of goodness reflecting that Essence. The purpose was not to balance an even-exchange of deposits and withdrawals to the 'First National Bank of God's Favor' but to gift the world with an overflowing Niagara of Grace-full blessings from the kingdom of God within. This is a major key in understanding Grace as a state of consciousness from which Grace-full blessings flow.

Jesus offered the fulfillment of the law through such teachings as: *"You have heard that it was said, 'An eye for an eye and a tooth for a tooth.' But I say unto you ... if anyone strikes you on the right cheek, turn to him the other also; and if any one would sue you and take your coat, let him have your cloak as well; and if any one forces you to go one mile, go with him two miles ... love your enemies, and pray for those who persecute you ... forgive, seventy times seven."* He never once offered an even-exchange idea as a *way* of life. He said, *"I am the way, and the truth, and the life ..."* (John, 14:6).

To paraphrase:

I, the Christ consciousness that lives in you, am the way, the truth, and the life, full of Grace and truth. I live in my Father, my Father lives in me, and I live in you. We inherited our Father's nature absent any ideas of even-exchange. Our Father loves because our Father is Love, and can only give unconditionally, true to the nature of Love—absent of the need for us to love God in return, for there is no God separate and apart from us. Our Father is abundance of all good, and can only give from that Essence without expectation of equal return. The return is the measure of more from the principle of abundance that always deals with more. Our Father is too pure to behold inequity, and forgives through the absence of the capacity to condemn. We are designed to be true to our nature as the way, the truth, and the life of God expressing without any need for even-exchange. Our nature is to give and live in the consciousness of Grace simply because we can't help ourselves—it is who we are.

The absence of the need for even-exchange fulfills the law, for all is given from Essence instead of expectations of return. Expectations are children of carnal mind. Giving from the nature of oneself, absent of expectations, is an inheritance of Gracemind.

Inventory of Soul

Here is a list of questions to inventory your motives,
actions, and content of mind. They will assist you in awakening
from any practice of even-exchange. They are for the purpose of
enlightenment and expansion of the state known as 'awake' in
Gracemind. Do not be afraid to answer honestly, for honesty is
a prerequisite of pure heart intention, and the scriptural promise
is that the pure in heart shall see God. Pure heart intention
precedes transformation, and transformation is the catalyst to
Grace awakening. If you find you are in the mental practice of
even-exchange in any of these areas, choose your Divine nature
of Peace, Love, and Joy as its replacement—the Mind energy
that awakens Gracemind in you.

Question: Do you function from even-exchange or
Gracemind in these situations?

*   What is your true feeling about going the extra
           mile? Do you do that naturally without reasoning or
           expectation, or do you do it because it is expected, and
           you feel guilty if you don't? Be sure to look in every
           area of your life with this one: work, relationships,
           cleaning, cooking, running errands, or serving in any
           capacity.

*   What is your response when someone has wronged
           you? Do you seek to get even and feel a need to expose
           their actions to others? Do you immediately call a
           friend and talk about it? Do you need your day in
           court?

*   Examine your gift giving. Is it without expectation of
           gratitude or the need for acknowledgment? Is it from a
           sense of abundance and joy, or is there some hesitation
           or fear associated with it? Can you give without the
           need for others to be deserving of the gift? This is a big
           one!

* Do you expect others to follow your advice or do it your way? When they don't, do you withhold your love in any way? Examine this dynamic in various relationships such as a spouse or significant other, friends, family members, the company you work for, or the employees who work for you.

* Look at your behavior while driving. Do you have a tendency to slip into road rage and a desire to get even, or are you centered in your peace in traffic, courteous even to someone who cuts you off?

* What is your reaction when others don't carry their load? Do you feel put upon or slide into the martyr role?

* How do you react to the programs you watch on TV? Are you satisfied when the villain gets his/her reward? Are you judgmental of the roles of the characters, hoping they will get what they deserve?

* What are your reactions as you read the newspaper?

* How do you decide on the amount to tip in a restaurant? Good service, good tip? Bad service, low tip or maybe no tip at all—just to be sure they get the message?

* Examine your hurt feelings. Are they justified by way of reason? Has someone abused you with words, physical violence, or by taking advantage of you? In your justification, do you need to get even or see they get their equal due?

* What is your attitude when returning telephone calls? Is it with joy in your heart, or is it from a sense of obligation? Ask yourself the same question regarding letters, Christmas cards, and invitations.

* When someone gives you a compliment, do you need to compliment them in return?

* If you forgive someone, do you expect them to forgive you?

* How do you pray? Is it with expectation for answered prayer exactly as you have asked? Are you telling God, seemingly separate from you, what to do and expecting God to do it your way in your time? Do you bargain with God, promising to do something in return for answered prayer?

* Have you created a god that tests you so you can evolve higher?

* Do you accept the cliché, "no pain, no gain," believing you must suffer in order to grow?

* In your expressions of love, do you expect love in return? Do you withhold it when it is not returned?

* How do you feel about those who have been proven guilty, crime and punishment, the events of 9/11, war, the holocaust, or Hitler? Do you feel a need to fight or join a cause—if so, from what motive?

* Perhaps you have evolved to the point you now say, "I don't need to get even, Captain Karma will get them." Hello! Wake up! What have you done here? Is this not subtle even-exchange? Your 911 call to Captain Karma does not send the rescue squad to relieve you from your judgment. True, the universe always balances itself as an effect of its own principles, but you are still clinging to a need to get even, and you will hang yourself for it.

A consciousness of Grace seeks not revenge or punishment for a deed expressed from fear, but rather to express the love the mind of fear could not see.

The subtleties of even-exchange consciousness are endless. This is just a short list. You are encouraged to keep a list of what you uncover as you stay awake to your motives and intentions. They are like a thief in the night and will grab you from behind if you are not careful. Then take what you find that is less than true to your nature, and offer it up as a gift of your most tenacious possession.

Mortal mind has a need to respond from a position of even-exchange because it feels as if some aspect of its freedom is being threatened. You may feel your very life is threatened, but remember, in truth, no aspect of your true nature or your life can possibly be extinguished.

The questions now in your heart may be, "BUT, what about …? What do I do about punishment for wrong? What do I do about people walking all over me or taking advantage of me? What is my responsibility as a parent? How do I stop someone from abusing me or my loved ones?"

Dearly Beloved, if you resort to even-exchange in any way, you have stooped to the level of the action. You are attempting to solve the problem at the level of the problem. This will not resolve anything, change any situation, or heal anyone. Return to Gracemind, and be still. Wait, take no thought! In the empty space of stilled awareness, the Essence of your Being will empower you to respond from Peace, Love, and Joy. This is the only way any situation or person will be restored to the experience of wholeness. Any other response becomes 'the accepted' by you and will multiply exponentially in *your* life.

Quantum physics has revealed there is more power in one cubic inch of empty space than the entire observable universe of matter. When your mind is *empty* of the need to get even, resting in its true nature, the power to transcend any problem will be revealed or will take care of the situation on its own. You may or may not be guided to 'do' anything. Love will be the determinant, for remember, Love is the moving force. Inherent within Love is the Divine wisdom that will discern precisely what aspect of Love is the correct prescription. Your non-attachment or lack of investment in outcome may be all that is needed to restore wholeness, or you may be Divinely guided to express Love in some form. You must wait for Love's impulse if you would remain in Grace consciousness.

What about 'causes?' Are you signed up because you are angry, see the injustice, and need to fix things? Or are you, instead, impulsed by Love's movement to *be* the Essence of Love in a particular situation? Have you totally surrendered to Love's embrace, allowing it to impulse your every thought, word, and deed in serving the cause? Has the eternal Reality of abundance as a perfect principle captured your heart to become the guiding light that serves those in need, or are you acting out of resentment for the waste in the world and the unfairness of poverty?

It is important to realize that any 'justified feelings' become the predominant thought frequencies that determine the metabolism of your soul and manifest as your challenges in life. These feelings become choice activators at the level of your vibration, finding a home in you and making choices for you without your conscious consent. You have consented at the level of the need for even-exchange, and whatever you wish for another is accepted as a wish for yourself. Because of the unified field of consciousness, consciousness cannot distinguish the difference between a thought, feeling, emotion, or action directed toward others, versus one that is directed toward self. Remember, 'it registers in your bones first.' Then, as it moves outward into Omnipresence, it will be accepted and made manifest by a vibratory correlate found in another. In other words, you accept at the level of everyone else who is insisting on the need for even-exchange. Thus, humanity continues to karma-lize, incarnation after incarnation.

While we are revisiting the subject of karma, let's remember what rocks its cradle—even-exchange. It is true that what you sow in thought, word, and deed—you reap in manifestation. As long as you continue to cradle the same intentions, motives,

attitudes, perceptions, feelings, emotions, judgments, and selfish desires anchored in even-exchange, you will experience your
life cycles as reruns. This is basic spiritual law, and will not
be mocked. The cradle breaks, and baby will fall out of karma
when the winds of Spirit blow in Grace. Your every breath is the
wind of Spirit. Be still and allow it (accept it) to take you out of
karma and into Graceland. I really think Elvis had the right idea.

As Grace continues to awaken deeper layers of
understanding, application of these eternal principles is not
optional. You know the truth, and blessed will you be if you
apply it. Once truth is known, there is a double-whammy of
return by the law of acceptance to those who do not apply
the truth according to Divine inheritance. This is because the
consciousness of ignorance carries with it innocence, whereas
the consciousness of 'knowing better,' when not applied,
generates a sense of guilt. Guilt registers in the mind as the
need for punishment, and on a very subtle level of acceptance,
you will multiply more punishment for yourself as well as more
opportunities to apply the principal with understanding. Woe be
unto you, Beloved; it behooves you to stay awake.

You are the Grace of God! It is time to *accept* this Reality
and lay down the burdens of your created experience of reality
and sense of separation. As God's Grace, you glorify this infinite
Presence as your very Being. All the Father is and has is yours
by Divine inheritance of your image and likeness of this Source.
Abundance the All through your *acceptance* and *freedom*. Claim
your Divinity as it is in Reality. Praise your Source as your very
own voice. Kneel before Thyself as God's Essence expressed.

As you advance in this study, you will recognize the
following truths:

> *Peace is to abundance as its source.*
> *Peace is the source of abundance.*
> *Love is to acceptance as its movement.*
> *Love is the movement of acceptance.*
> *Joy is to freedom as its wings.*
> *Joy is the wings of freedom.*

Chapter Three

The Awakening

Chapter 3

The Awakening

The Master Mind circle:
Master Mind
Verity
Gracemind—Spiritual DNA
Serving—Miracles
Observer—Acceptance
Resurrection—Ascension
God As Me

Mortal Mind
Victim
Separation—Duality
Judgment
No Control
Anthropomorphic God

Mind
Virgin
Essence—Unity
All That Is—'I'-deas
Being—Eternal Life
Peace, Love, Joy
I is God

Mystic Mind
Vessel
Surrender
Holy Spirit Baptism
Crucifixion—Integration
Merging Will
God In Me

Metaphysical Mind
Venturer
Seeker—Reason
Choice—Discernment
Transformation—Change
God Thru Me

The journey of awakening is the story of the prodigal son in you, which I prefer to reference as *the prodigal butterfly*. Guided by the Wings of Spirit and the promise of Love's keeping coded within your soul, your transformation is assured.

The butterfly begins its life as a tiny egg about the size of the head of a pin. "*As the time of hatching nears ... the eggshell darkens and becomes almost transparent. ...The larva chews through the eggshell and emerges into the world.*" This is where we will enter our dialogue on Grace awakening.

The wormlike butterfly larva or caterpillar looks nothing like a winged adult. After hatching from the egg, the young caterpillar spends most of its time eating leaves and gaining weight ...The butterfly larva,

*or caterpillar, spends most of its time eating, digesting
its food, and growing. The caterpillar undergoes
several molts of its skin until it becomes full grown
and has accumulated enough body mass to carry it
through the entire life cycle, including the adult phase.
... Caterpillars consume huge quantities of leaves—and
they are very specific about which plants they will
eat. Most will eat plants from only a single species or
genus, called the host plant for that caterpillar; it will
die rather than feed on others.*

*The larva repeatedly outgrows its skin, which
splits and is shed. At the end of its growth period, the
caterpillar stops eating and finds a good place to molt
into the next stage. It spins a small pad of silk and
attaches itself to it, hanging upside down, immobile.
The larval skin then splits one last time, revealing the
pupa.*

*The caterpillar then enters the pupal stage, when
it neither feeds nor moves. From the outside, it appears
as though the pupa, also known as the chrysalis, is
resting. In reality, though, the larval tissues completely
break down and reorganize within the pupal skin.
...Inside the skin of the pupa, or chrysalis, the most
dramatic part of the metamorphosis takes place.*

*When the butterfly is fully formed, the pupal
case splits and the butterfly emerges. The butterfly
first expels its meconium, metabolic waste products
that have accumulated during the pupal stage. The
butterfly's wings are initially soft and shriveled, but
they expand and harden within a few hours. ...It then
expands its ...wings—by pumping them full of blood
before flying off. ... It has no time to waste—adults of
most species live for only a few weeks."*

The story of the butterfly can be found on the website of the
American Museum of Natural History:
http://www.amnh.org/exhibitions/butterflies/metamorphosis.html

The above illustration is a metaphor that correlates to spiritual evolution through different degrees of Grace awakening in consciousness from Mortal Mind to Mind itself. Through each phase of this awakening, veils of contextualized content wrapped in soul memory dissolve into the nothingness from which they emerged. These veils simply disappear much like the evaporated caterpillar in the final metamorphosing process.

We will use the circular illustration at the beginning of this chapter and the butterfly metaphor to emphasize clarity within our dialogue. I call the circular diagram, 'the M&M's of consciousness evolution.' It is a little sweeter journey that way. The *'Ms'* stand for: Mortal Mind, Metaphysical Mind, Mystical Mind, Master Mind, and ultimately, Mind. Each phase of this journey is important, for it is an enabler to the next and assists in the shifting sands of mind embracing the creative process.

You may wonder if it is possible to simply awaken in the twinkling of an 'I' instead of going through these progressive portals? Yes, it is possible, but for most spiritual seekers this is not the experience. One of the reasons is, the Mind energy of the total awakened state is such an intensified high frequency that the physical, mental, and emotional systems would self-destruct if the awakening happened all at once. In a gradual ascension, there is a soft awakening as though from a deep sleep. This is the way of Grace—the arms of sweet embrace.

Christ taught life was designed to be a journey into the unknown that requires faith and trust in the infinite presence of Love. His life story shows us it was designed to be companioned by the Holy Spirit as the inner teacher. As this journey unfolds, it is revealed as an adventure into worlds within worlds of the vast ocean of consciousness unfolding greater and greater depths, dimensions, and gifts of Grace. *"In my Father's house are many mansions ..."* (John 14:2). Your destiny is eternal life in Christ consciousness. This is your fulfillment—the Grace of God unfolding itself in a world of infinite expression. The journey of discovery is an adventure of priceless treasure.

Grace consciousness does not find more value in the journey's end than it does the journey. Like the river flowing freely, being gravitationally drawn from place to place, however long and winding, and allowing the stepping stones of life their place within its journey, the river acquires a greater gift: the joy of the journey and the thrill of the unexpected blessing at the turn of each river's bend on its return to Source. This is the journey of Grace Awakening.

As you become more conscious of this journey, it will be helpful to begin a personal journal, divided into sections which reflect each of the stages of your own awakening. There will be events, memories, and situations companioned by deep feelings, emotions, and thought patterns that are reflective of each stage. Journaling from the heart of memory is often very beneficial during certain times of the spiritual journey. It serves the purpose of identifying what is real from the unreal, separating the wheat from the tares of Reality. There may also come a time when journaling has fulfilled its purpose, and you may feel guided to stop that practice.

It is important to note that movement from one stage into another is not always linear. You may often fall back into a state previously traveled while at the same time traveling through a more expanded one. This is natural and as much a part of designed evolution as is advancement.

Let's begin this Grace awakening understanding of your destiny by examining the conditions and mind-sets of each phase of the journey.

Mortal Mind

Let us begin by identifying layers of awareness from the phase in the awakening known as Mortal Mind. This phase ultimately culminates in a wake-up call from Spirit to exit the land of Fantasia wherein you travel in circles with your eyes myopically focused in earth and your feet moving you about. The image of the caterpillar is perfect.

Reality, to your awareness at this stage, is confined to what is directly before you, around you, and beneath you. Struggle and strife are an everyday occurrence, with the focus being mainly on supplying the needs of the physical. There is a tremendous sense of separation from all that is seen, paradoxed by a deep yearning to be an accepted part of your localized world. You seek to find comfort and stability from what you observe. Loneliness, striving to possess what is seen, efforting to make things happen, coveting, driven by the need of the ego to be in control, yet feeling everything is out of control—this is the constant struggle during this phase of the journey. For the most part, you look out upon the world and feel controlled and ultimately victimized by it.

Judgment is the food for thought consumed and the indigestion of the soul at the level of Mortal Mind. It continues to reinforce your world of duality, mirroring to you absolute proof. Judgment is the response to your sense of victimization and the fuel for the motivation of getting even. You believe your survival depends upon it. Your need to control is paramount, for fear of annihilation is all consuming. From this position, life is identified as living in sin or suffering. This world is most certainly out to get you. Woe is me!

If you stay in this vibrational frequency of awareness, you are destined to accumulate and experience trials and tribulation, confusion, frustration, and, most of all, a wavering faith and little understanding of the unity of all life—let alone your position within that unity.

Mortal Mind is governed by karma, reaping a constant repetitive crop from the seeds of mental content not aligned with the nature of Being which have been sown in the conscious and subconscious levels of Mind. In this stage you are continually waiting for something to happen or trying to make something happen according to your *perception* of what life should be and who you *think* you are. The sense of victimization mounts and gathers memories to prove to brain mind that victimization is a way of life, and feelings less than love are justified.

Even in a crowd, Mortal Mind feels a sense of aloneness. There is a deep need to belong, and you try to fit in and become a clone of who and what you see. You want to be a part of the herd or the tribe and cluster in selective groups you surmise will nourish you—similar to the caterpillar being "*very specific about which plants they will eat. Most will eat plants from only a single species or genus, called the host plant for that caterpillar; it will die rather than feed on others.*" This is a metaphor for the attraction to specific religious persuasions and collective perceptions of Reality.

The concept of God is usually introduced at this stage, but God is perceived as being 'out there' somewhere in some anthropomorphic garb. You appease Him to grant you immunity from your sins and bless you with His forgiveness. You strive to be and do good, but no matter how sincere your efforts, you are told and ultimately feel you are a sinner trapped in a futile and eternal state of the need for repentance. You also have your gaze turned outward with your cup held high to be filled by this God who lives in a heaven somewhere 'up there.'

The prodigal caterpillar finally comes to itself with a cry that rises from a heart of desperation, "God help me!" Begging and beseeching become the mode of prayer. This is the catalyst for awakening. It is the impulse of Grace calling from within to accept more of what it is, to know and expand awareness, and to release more of the fragrance of Being. God hears the call, because no matter *how* God is perceived or *where* God is perceived to be, the truth remains—God is awakening within your humanity through ways and means unknown as yet to Mortal Mind awareness.

How does one get to this state? That is endless speculation I will leave to other authors to fantasize, analyze, and theorize. All you need to know is when you are in it, and that, by the Grace of God, you ain't-a-gonna stay there.

This state is most definitely not your predominant awareness, Beloved, or you would not be reading this book, but every once in a while, even though you have evolved to more advanced understandings, remnants of Mortal Mind awareness surface from your conditioned memory. When this happens, you may feel victimized and the need to get even. There may even be times you still fall to your knees, begging for help from a God you feel has abandoned you. That's perfectly normal.

Then along comes John—John the Baptist, the metaphysical voice inside you crying in the wilderness, "repent!"

Metaphysical Mind

This stage usually announces its arrival during a traumatic experience that brings you to your knees, or when you have a deep questioning in your heart about some spiritual understanding. Your belief system may have become challenged, or your world may feel like it is falling apart. Your cry sounds something like: "There must be something more than this, or surely there is a way out of my problem. Please help me Lord!" Sometimes, a sense of desperation is felt as a deep longing to know who you truly are. "Who am I, what am I, why am I?" Your call for assistance is ushered up to God either in the form of a desperate cry for help or an earnest prayer from your heart. God answers your call through a so-called 'chance meeting' of someone who introduces you to a whole new way of thinking, or maybe someone knocks at your door with a book in hand or an invitation for you to attend a gathering. Your eye may be captured by a flyer on the bulletin board at the grocery store or at work, announcing a workshop or seminar that sounds interesting. You feel compelled to go. For the first time you have the ears to hear. You respond to the impulse from God, initiated from your confusion and suffering. The impulse is to "repent," for the kingdom of *change* is at hand.

You hear a new voice within that calls for repentance, a change of awareness, a change in the way of thinking, feeling, and acting. You are being asked to be willing to be metaphysically baptized—cleansed of the error of your ways and perceptions. You are being asked to be willing to be transformed by the renewal of your Mortal Mind awareness and awakened to the Reality that you have a choice.

Metaphysical Mind is a stage of repentance, not from an awareness of Mortal Mind which feels itself to be a hopeless 'sinner,' but from the realization that you are, in some way, a participant of the world's reflection, and a change within you is needed. The metaphysical meaning of 'repent' is to change your

way of thinking, feeling, and responding. You are being asked
to change your thoughts, feelings, actions, and perceptions of
who you are, and to shift your understanding of your relationship
to the world and to God. The journey accelerates. Movement is
felt within the soul. There seems to be a light at the end of the
tunnel. You realize there is something more than meets the eye.

At this point you emerge with a pile of books in your
arms and a sign-up sheet for every workshop being offered in
metaphysical circles. Friends of the past seem to go 'poof' in the
night, and circumstances, relationships, and situations show up
with new faces. Portals within mind open to new realizations,
understandings, and metaphors of truth. It is a new day dawning,
and your heart begins to lift out of the ashes.

In this stage you break away from the old tribe and join a
new one—the tribe of reason, evaluation, and logic. It is a time
of yard-selling old content of mind and buying new stuff. The
old is exchanged for the new—negative for positive. You are
putting new wine into new wineskins. You feel great, for you are
taking control, and your life is reflecting positive change.

Unbeknownst to you—the seeker—at this phase of the
journey, that which you are seeking is seeking you. Any call
for help serves as an invitation for the Holy Spirit to begin a
descent into the depths of your soul to uproot all illusions of
consciousness. This is scripturally referenced as being baptized
by water. It is a cleansing initiated for the renewal of the mind
or a changed way of thinking. Mortal Mind awareness is giving
birth to Metaphysical Mind awareness—the awareness of one
who seeks to understand self and find meaning and purpose in
life. This will spawn an intense and long period of searching and
conscious awakening.

It is important to recognize that movement from one level
of awareness into the next is always precipitated by a paradigm
shift of mind and heart. At the core of the shift is the movement
of God's Grace through the activity of the Holy Spirit for the
purpose of awakening the prodigal into the awareness of the
Essence of Being. God stirs to quicken that awareness within
itself as you! In Mortal Mind awareness, the cry, "Help me,

God," in any form, is the catalyst for that movement. This is a Grace-full movement of Love.

In Metaphysical Mind awareness, the innate desire to know, to seek, and to find the truth is the quickening agent for the paradigm shift. This desire is genetically initiated from the spiritual DNA of the soul which impulses the Will of God into meaningful expression for the purpose of generating a new life in Christ. In other words, the cry, "Help me, God," and the impulse to know, seek and find, serve as different means to the same end—knowing oneness in God. It is all for good and for the destined awakening of the soul. You will be able to see these subtle movements as you continue on in the journey.

Metaphysical Mind is a stage of being "born again," again—and again in hot pursuit of the truth and the meaning of life. In this stage you learn the power of positive thinking. You begin to grasp the transforming power of holding loving thoughts of forgiveness, compassion, and oneness. You are encouraged to surrender judgment in exchange for discernment. Forgiveness is your daily bread, and you feel the shackles of your mind falling to the wayside as you practice changes of thought, word, and deed. Your searching soul turns inward, seeking to find the indwelling Spirit. There is a consciousness shift from victim to venturer which impulses you into many dimensions of the inner worlds. You are becoming a conscious co-creator, and for the first time begin to see there are no victims, only volunteers, through the gift of freewill choice of thoughts, feelings, and actions.

Metaphysical Mind is a stage of exploring many types of meditation and of holding affirmations of truth as a practiced focus. Prosperity is paramount as a goal of every aspect of life. It is a time of study, taking classes, workshops, and seminars. There is an insatiable appetite for reading and digesting truth. Like a dry sponge, you—the seeker—soak up every spiritual teaching that is thrown your way. You may even flit from one church to another or one philosophy to another as if you are garage sale hopping.

The analytical aspect of mind works overtime trying
to fit spirituality into a neat, little, tidy package. It craves an
explanation for everything and sincerely desires to understand. It
wants to get a handle on this 'truth thing,' be right, and have the
one and only answer to the mystery of life and self. Intellectual
knowledge in relationship to meaning is valued above all else as
the "pearl of great price."

"Do-do, do-do" ... the opening theme of the Twilight Zone
seems appropriate. The unexplained fascinates the exploring
Metaphysical Mind. The paranormal, out of body experiences,
near death experiences, flying saucers, space beings, crop circles,
crystals, astrology, and hierarchies are of interest. Anatomy of
the Spirit, soul, body, chakra system, vegetarianism, yoga, Reiki,
massage, chanting, sound therapy, and on and on, present endless
possibilities of exploration. Like the child who has found new
freedom to walk, talk, and choose for itself, the metaphysician
is out to experience it all. Nothing's wrong with this; it's natural,
evolutionary, educative, and enlightening, but it won't satisfy the
soon-to-come, deeper yearning of the soul to know God. If the
metaphysician is not careful, too much of this type exploration
can lead to more illusions and a greater sense of separation than
before. This is the John the Baptist stage that can result in too
much *intellectual* pursuit causing one to lose one's head. When
your head is ahead, its time to reposition.

The following poem was written by a dear friend of mine. It
captures the experience of being in the Metaphysical Mind phase
of the journey of awakening. Enjoy!

New Age Burnout

By Light Roper

Hurry, scurry, run about.
What if there's a workshop
And I'm left out?
For years I have been on a wild tirade,
Trying to master every "trick of the trade."
I'm not pointing fingers or judging my brother;

It's just that someone keeps inventing another.

There's acupuncture, acupressure, reflexology,
Polarity therapy, aroma therapy, and iridology.
There's left brain, right brain, kinesiology,
Transition, nutrition, and don't forget astrology.

Another brochure reads, "Come to my Session.
I'm offering hypnosis and past life regression."

There's naturopathic, homeopathic, and macrobiotics,
Encouraging us to say goodbye to antibiotics!

We've got mustard greens, adzuki beans, wakame, and kombu,
Soy-burgers, miso soup, sprouts, and tofu.
There's rebirthing, Reiki, and NLP,
Sweat Lodges, vision quests, and sexuality.

A thing of the past is L.S.D.
Who needs it when we've got E.S.T.?

Crystal healing, psychic healing, therapeutic touch,
Swedish massage, Shiatsu, Rolfing, and such.

Come for a weekend of complete transformation,
With Yogi Masters, spiritual attunements, and meditation.

Rejuvenate, regenerate, revitalize.
Dance, chant, breathe, and exercise.
Everyone seems to have "just the solution"
The rest of us need for our evolution.

Take my name from your list please.
I have passed my test.
My inner guru says, "let me rest."

You may well ask, "What purpose does this stage serve?" It
quickens the aspirant to the awareness of the freewill choice for

thoughts, feelings, and actions, and it empowers the aspirant with the capability to accept responsibility for his/her consequences. It reveals many clues that will lead to the portal of the inward journey of the prodigal's return home; it awakens the mystery of the All-in-all; it grants glimpses into the unity of the soul with all life. The path of the metaphysician also provides a period for developing ego strength and self assurance that will be necessary temporary companions in order to venture deeper and deeper into the chambers of the heart.

Metaphysical Mind is very committed to looking into the mirror of life's relationships. It explores the inner domains of the subconscious and outer conditions of current situations to determine how they reflect false perceptions, worn out tapes, or positions of mind incongruent with new found truth. Metaphysical Mind is thrilled to find the law of cause and effect and to realize it is its impersonal user. It isn't easy holding all those affirmations and getting mind to cooperate, but the aspirant is swimming upstream, spawning in new territory, and mesmerized by the new scenery. These are very beneficial supplies to carry as the journey expands.

One of the gifts gathered in this phase will be your ability to see the world as an infinite opportunity for choice in a system reflecting the unity of opposites and paradoxes. You will be introduced to the concept of non-duality, but it will be much later before the depth of this truth is fully accepted. Intellectually, you can see your neighbor as yourself and all as One. God is working through you, awakening, transforming, and healing. Unconditional love is giving birth in stages. God is now felt as the flow of an imminent Presence, and you don't feel nearly as alone. Many of your questions are answered. It is a good time!

The key characteristics of Metaphysical Mind are: (1) a sincere searching for truth; (2) a willingness to apply the truth as it is understood; (3) the capacity to take responsibility for one's experience of life; and (4) the willingness to change and forgive.

There will be some signals that usually accompany the culmination of this phase of the journey when it is about to fulfill its purpose, and a new portal is about to open. I list a few of them here so you will not be taken by surprise, lose faith, or feel any pain when asked to shed your skin once again. *"The larva repeatedly outgrows its skin, which splits and is shed."*

1. You feel you have arrived, or have become the conquering hero/heroine.
2. That feeling will subtly shift to a desire to *know and merge with* the *One* within you that has made that conquering possible.
3. The pit of subconscious content appears to be endless, and your fascination with the 'witch hunt' (inner uncovery) becomes depressing and finally boring. You get really bored with *your* never ending story and the stories of your friends.
4. Answers to your questions seem to turn around and become questions at deeper levels.
5. There is restlessness, uneasiness, and a stirring of energies within you that you can't explain.
6. You feel like you cannot take another step or search any further. You have no desire to read another book, take another class, or explore another path. You just want to *know* the truth and *be* remembered as its expression.

Mystic Mind

Just when you think you are at the peak of the wave in the ocean, towering above your oceanite buddies, you may crash into the shore and feel yourself being sucked back into the endless sea. The mystic is born, and all illusions of being in control now shatter. The self you thought you had discovered through metaphysical understanding may experience a sense of crucifixion. The nocturnal dark may seem to shadow the *Son* Light. It could be a long night indeed. This stage has the potential for being the longest phase of the journey, for the mirrors begin to shatter, and the antichrist, the ego, holds on for dear life. The length and the degree of darkness will be determined by the tenaciousness of you, the aspirant, attempting to hold on to illusions and error beliefs resistant to the true nature of Being.

Memories you thought were healed swim to the surface of your awareness with unveiled faces. Long searched-for answers you gleaned as a metaphysician now become questions, and you may feel lost in an ocean of inner turmoil. The mystic mermaid feels compelled to swim deep to escape the raging storms at the surface. Little does s/he know something beyond wildest imagining is about to be discovered.

Diving through surfaced waves of anger, resentment, and pain, affirmations that no longer seem to produce, concepts of truth, and cellular memories of hurt and trauma, the mystic mermaid swims deeper and deeper trying to escape. S/he realizes old states of mind were not really healed, only sent into remission. S/he thought s/he had conquered, but now feels defeated. All s/he wants is a respite from the thoughts, feelings, and emotions that are surfacing from myriad lifetimes of existence. S/he aches for truth, absolute, yet is caught in a web of the relative—seaweed of the mind. Surely there is a Reality beyond any seeming reality s/he can create?

No longer content to swim in the ocean, s/he longs to *become* the ocean, merged with the Source. Like the fish looking for the water, s/he cries, "Where is the water?" S/he realizes s/he doesn't really want just a better life; s/he is passionate for God as life itself. S/he hungers and thirsts for the sea which s/he is. Deeper s/he goes, deeper and deeper into the abyss of the endless content of the sea—memories, feelings, lifetimes of 'stuff' floating to the surface, until finally, from pure exhaustion, s/he abandons the search.

The caterpillar then enters the pupal stage, when it neither feeds nor moves. From the outside, it appears as though the pupa, also known as the chrysalis, is resting ... It spins a small pad of silk and attaches itself to it, hanging upside down, immobile.

The metamorphosing of the mystic is long and lonely for most. The mystical stage feels as though your world has turned upside down, and you are totally immobile. Your previously acquired spiritual tools don't seem to work any more, and there is no interest in a new set. It is an inner journey with seemingly no companions; a journey in unfamiliar territory, scary and threatening—there are no bridges, boats, or 911 phone lines offering assistance. There are no rules, maps, or anything familiar, and nothing feels solid. There is an earthquake in the soul, and the building blocks of the spiritual journey seem to be crumbling into dust.

You are exhausted from *reasoning* your way into expressing unconditional love in thought, word, and deed. You crave to *be Love without the need for reason*, serve without the desire for recognition, and pole vault the need to judge in order for forgiveness to become an antiquated exercise.

Your friends and relatives are concerned about you. Some think you have gone off the deep end. Now, even your metaphysical friends think you are weird, and some of them exit your life. Your mind and body are experiencing energies you never felt before, and there is a longing for *home*. There are times of weeping for no apparent reason, and bursts of joy come out of nowhere. Sometimes you laugh and cry at the same time. If your friends think you are weird, you think yourself weirder. Nothing seems familiar, especially you to yourself.

You are obsessed with spiritual house-cleaning, and your mind craves empty spaces. You desire above all else to be used as an empty vessel of Love. "Here I am Lord, use me," is your prayer. You pray for surrender to consume you as your ego battles to hold on. You have become a paradox of paradox, intuitively wanting to die so you can live. You experience yourself as a warrior going through the battle of Armageddon, a metaphor for the dark night of the soul.

Our history is filled with prodigals who have gone before us—even Christ experienced the dark night. Accounts are plentiful, and I encourage you to make their stories your companion if this is the stage of your awakening.

The greatest companion of all is the truth that you are not alone, and that what you are experiencing is a temporary metamorphosing to greater freedom. Not only that, it is the chrysalis of the portal into the kingdom of Grace consciousness. "Don't worry, be happy." Rest and be still. *Allow* the shift to take place. You cannot affect the shift no matter how desperately you try. You are being completely broken down and reorganized. It is happening on its own. You might as well surrender completely into the coffin of your cocoon, which in truth is the manger of the Christ child, of Gracemind being born in you. The only thing you can do is surrender and trust! Embrace what I call the S.T.A.R. system—Surrender, Trust, Allow, and Rest.

S.T.A.R.

SURRENDER all. Release and let go of any attachment you may have to anything, anyone, or any situation, positive or negative. Within your spiritual DNA, tenaciousness does not exist. Move into trust activating Divine Will.

> **TRUST** God. Trust Principle. Trust your Divine Destiny. Trust your spiritual DNA. Trust Divine Will. Trust *from* the nature of Trust you are!

> **ALLOW/Accept** the Divine Plan for your life. Accept your Divinity. Accept everything that happens to you and through you. Accept others' choices and the consequences of those choices. Allow diversity. Accept polarities.

> **REST** in every phase, layer, and state of your Being. Rest in your Infinite Self. Rest in doing. Rest in Being. Rest at the center of every motion. Take a Sabbath from attachment. Rest!

And you thought there was change during the stage of Metaphysical Mind awakening! *"Inside the skin of the pupa, or chrysalis, the most dramatic part of the metamorphosis takes place."* The mystic is being asked to surrender all in order to be transformed into the Master—the butterfly within. Mystic Mind yearns for God awareness, and God awareness only. Any perception that shadows that knowing must be made shadowless by the radiation of the *Son*.

> *Mystics are the ones who hunger and thirst after righteousness, as the Bible puts it, the ones who yearn for continued or increased union with the other reality they themselves feel is the real reality—the reality which heals and makes all things new again. Their yearning is their most distinctive mark and has been called by some a "deep burning wound," because it propels them toward the transcendent nature of life much as a lover is drawn toward the object of his love. The term is also descriptive of the slow and painful completion process of joining totally with, or being in, the transcendent state—a process that should not be confused with psychological development. The latter is a matter of self-understanding, self-acceptance and personal integration. The former involves itself with self-forgetting, the disappearance of the self into mysterious union with God, the absolute, the transcendent aspect of Reality, the Tao.*

Sinetar, Marsha. 1986. *Ordinary People as Monks and Mystics*, p. 7. New York: Paulist Press.

The path of the Mystic can be experienced as painful and all consuming because of the degree of selflessness and surrender that is required. But it can also be the most glorious experience on the spiritual journey if the aspirant thoroughly understands the metamorphosing processes of crucifixion, integration, and Holy Spirit baptism/regeneration that is taking place. When clearly understood and fully accepted as the movement of Grace, this stage of the journey embraces the possibility of being the opposite of the dark night of the soul. It has the potential to be the one stage absent of all pain and suffering and instead filled with liberation, enlightenment, and instant awakening. What makes the latter a possibility is integration and application of what is required to navigate in this stage—total and complete *surrender* embraced through *acceptance*. But, because the Mystic often holds the concept that surrender is a relinquishment of some valued perception, belief, relationship, or coveted thing, the possibility of pain-free journeying through this stage usually eludes Mystic Mind.

The mystic is being asked to surrender all ideas of self control which have given birth from a sense of separation, all concepts of a self identity separate from God—all ego states. Awareness is being stripped naked of all its illusions for the purpose of awakening the awareness of the One, the eternal I. 'I' is the only One, the only Reality, so what is there to release or let go? Pain and suffering can only be experienced by one who thinks there is something *real* to release, give up, or have torn asunder. How simple can this phase of the journey be? There is nothing to lose, only the eternal Reality of who you are to accept. Be still and know, 'I' is God—NO Separation, and the only One in control.

What I have just offered you is the pain-free way of Grace awakening. If you continue to suffer, it is because of the degree of attachment to your egoic illusions. Pain is the effect of a long period of identifying areas of consciousness that present the illusion of separation. Once the illusion is discovered, the mystic is consumed by the desire to surrender, let go, and empty the conscious and subconscious of the content of this debris. The need to let go, empty, and do it yourself is a carry-over from Metaphysical Mind processing. **The only way to let go of that which does not exist is to accept that which does.** The pain free way is to *accept* the Peace, Love, and Joy of God *you* truly IS! If this is true, and it is, would not the awareness of your Divinity consume all egoic perceptions unlike itself, automatically dissolving them into the nothing from which they temporally emerged as content of mind?

The dark night of the soul is simply the dark night of the ego. It is the *Phantom of the Opera*, the *Ghost of Christmas Past*. It serves only to reveal your beauty, your love, your peace, and your joy as soon as you are ready to accept yourself as the Beloved.

It may sound to you as though I am contradicting myself by telling you there is nothing to surrender, and then saying you must surrender all illusions. This is definitely a paradox that needs to be reconciled by your brain mind. Do not see surrender as a relinquishment or letting go of any 'thing'—see surrender as *acceptance* of the nature of your Essence. Your pain is the effect of attachment to the 'nothing.'

You surrender and surrender until there is no need to surrender, until something snaps wide awake in your awareness and *knows* that what is being released is an illusion, not true, not real. The instant *no-thing* is recognized as nothing, the mind breathes an 'ah-ha' sigh of freedom, and it is finished! It is finished because the mind finally *accepts* the truth of Being.

Through spiritual practices such as Contemplative Prayer, the Grace Prayer, or any prayer of the heart that yearns only for God awareness, the mystic becomes an empty vessel, purified and cleansed. The awareness dawns that Grace is functioning, integrating mind with heart—turning the tables in the temple of consciousness over to reveal any false idols that may be lingering as inhibitors to the realization of the true nature of Being. In your fallen state of 'asleep' you have accumulated nightmares of false ideas about who you are. The mystical phase of your journey is about surrendering any false perceptions and awakening to the already perfected state.

One of my favorite books is *Dialogue on Awakening* by Tom & Linda Carpenter. Read the following paragraph over several times. It is a spiritual 'I' opener:

> *The state of your Being remains forever unaltered.*
> *That is why it is easy for me to assure you that the*
> *reconnection you seek will come, and this quandary*
> *that seems to be overwhelming you at the moment will*

fall away. You have never changed. You are as the Father created you, but you just haven't let yourself remember it. You may also be very thankful that there is nothing you can do to change it. What could you fear if you kept repeating to yourself, "There is nothing I can do to alter my Being." Your mind is powerful enough to keep your attention from it, but it has absolutely no power to change it.

Carpenter, Tom & Linda. 1992. *Dialogue on Awakening,* p.5. Port Ludlow: The Carpenters' Press.

Your true nature can never be changed or altered. You can awaken to it but never make it into something it is not already. As confirmation of this truth, I often hear these words when I still my mind to the Presence: "*I cannot be what I am not. I cannot not be what I am.*"

The mystic emerges from the cocoon of darkness integrated as the caterpillar surrendered within the butterfly, transformed into the awareness of the Essence of God, transparent and flowing as a vessel of Light, Love, and Life into the free world. The sense of separation was the final thread imprisoning Gracemind to the cocoon of Mystic Mind. The Master/Gracemind is resurrected, and the works that Christ did you now do also, Beloved. You are the Grace of God awakened—the miracle minded serving Essence!

The Master Mind

"*When the butterfly is fully formed, the pupal case splits and the butterfly emerges. The butterfly first expels its meconium, metabolic waste products that have accumulated during the pupal stage. The butterfly's wings are initially soft and shriveled, but they expand and harden within a few hours. It then expands its wings—by pumping them full of blood before flying off. ... It has no time to waste—adults of most species live for only a few weeks.*"

In your totally surrendered/accepting state, your metamorphosis completes itself. You, as you previously understood yourself, do not exist any more. Your metamorphosis is destined from the seed code of your original design that has been made ready through an evolutionary spiraling journey of Grace awakening. The Master that is written in your design awakens as Gracemind, a new creature in Christ. Totally pure in heart you are the verity (eternal truth) of God.

The newly emerged Master is recognized as the knower, the known, and the knowing. The *idea* of oneness was Pabulum compared to the *experience* of oneness. The Master knows itself to be the observer, the observed, and the observing. S/he accepts the All from the awareness of being All. There is still relationship, but not as separate or outside of all that is. Relationship is more like the companionship of the notes to a symphony which have become the song. Spirit, soul, and body flow as one harmonic symphony of Gracemind awareness.

The baptism is finished. The battle of Armageddon is over. Healing has taken place. The soul is quiet. There is no more searching or seeking, no need to remember or be remembered, nothing to surrender, and no one to surrender to. There is no desire to force change in the world or in others. There is no need for tribes or companions, for the cosmos has familyed itself in the Master. The Master lives from pure bliss as God's heart awakened. This is freedom's flight.

The concept of death is no more, for that was the survival mechanism of the ego which can no longer be found. There are no needs, wants, or yearnings. Everything needed is provided from the Essence of the Master.

Having made all things new, Christ now sits upon the throne of consciousness. Christ, the Master Mind, is complete, and you recognize yourself as one in Christ. There are no delusions of separation, no fears—no bruises or shadows left on the soul, no scars in the heart, and no hidden manuscripts. The soul is clean. The mind and heart are cradled as one, knowing God is not just in you, God is expressing as you. The second coming has taken place. Christ has taken you to itself and come again as you, now living from Grace & truth as Gracemind awareness.

Acceptance is the focus of your peace, and all thoughts, feelings, and movements of action are impelled and compelled by the Will of God, willing itself into expression. Peace, Love, and Joy are the natural flow of the waving ocean of your consciousness. The living water has been found, and the mermaid has disappeared into it.

The mind is empty of content, resting in the eternal bliss of always. *Always* is known to be all the now there is. There is no more searching, no efforting, and no possessing. Your heart of acceptance has replaced desire, and God is glorified through your manifestations. The world you see is unified, for it is seen through your unified Mind, the single I. You are in complete control through no need to control, for you accept the Will of God which is your own. Joy is your effortless state of Mind. You have been totally regenerated and transformed by the Love of God you are. Reality is the world holding you, and you no longer swim or crawl, but are free to soar and fly. This is ascension while still remaining in sweet Earth.

In the infant stages of this new you, your wings are "*soft and shriveled.*" This is an accurate description of the newly emerged Being. It will take some time to adjust to this new Self. A time apart a while longer will definitely be needed; a time for *the blood (new life) of Christ* to fill your new wings. When your imprisoned splendor emerges, it is in the spring of its seasons, fragile, tender, and totally other. The time will not yet have come for you to begin your flight. This adjustment may take months or even years.

Master Mind consciousness is only awake in a minute minority of our species, and, when it occurs, most of these rare butterflies are never seen or heard from again, for nothing in this world calls their name. They hold the portal open for the rest of us from the Essence of their *Being*, awakened. If it is written in their original design, some return to the masses to teach or guide for a brief amount of time. "*... adults of most species live for only a few weeks.*" The fully awakened Christ of Jesus was with the masses for only a short period of time, and so were most of the other butterflies who came after him. But, if you ever encounter such a rare beauty, you will be speechless with awe and wonder. When you see one, be sure to remember this great truth: *'There as the Grace of God go I.'*

How long will we remain in Master consciousness? Nobody knows. Is there something beyond this? Well, of course. There is and always will be more, *more* of the Grace of God expanding. What will that look like? God only knows. I can speculate and call it *the* state of *Mind*, infinite, virgin Mind. I can identify it as the state of Eternal Beingness as God awareness. I can surmise we will be a perfect body of Light, but exactly what form that will take I have no heavenly idea. But I can assure you there is more because of the nature of Grace itself; more is your destiny and mine as we continue on the soul's journey of eternal life in the Gracemind consciousness of Christ.

Look back and carefully examine the circle diagram at the beginning of this chapter. Notice how each phase overlaps into the other one and connects in the center circle of Mind. As you awaken in each of these circles, it will be comforting to realize that when you are in one phase, you also have one I/eye in the other. One phase should not be coveted over another, for they are all expansions of *Gracemind* that determine 'readiness.' They each contain necessary components of consciousness to be mastered. Mortal Mind contains the potential for awakening; Metaphysical Mind contains the potential for reason and understanding; Mystical Mind contains the potential for total surrender through acceptance; Master Mind contains the awareness of unity; and Mind *is* All.

I have not written any lengthy description of Mind awareness, for at this phase of my own evolution it would be impossible. I have written some descriptive words that emerged from silence that point us in the direction of Mind awareness, for as I stated earlier, I recognize the power of words to point us in the direction of their Essence. Each word stands alone as descriptive of Mind, or they can be read as a collective. They will, in some Always, perhaps in another world, absorb us in all ways!

Mind
Is
All
Ineffable Ineffableness,
Pure Silence
As
Virgin Unity,
Love, Peace, Joy,
of
Original Design,
Always
Pure Thought,
Substanceless Substance,
Sourceless Source,
Grace of Grace,
Life of Life
Virgin
Is
I

(Read from top to bottom, then from bottom to top—the original design of the eternal butterfly is revealed)

Chapter Four

The Mirroring

Chapter 4

The Mirroring

The glory of the Lord stands before each mirrored Self
to reflect its own image.
Look with the eyes of the heart. See your own Idea.
Clothe it not.

The message of Grace awakening through the stages mentioned in chapter three can all be found in the teachings of Jesus. In order to find them you must look deeply into the awareness of his consciousness as expressed in his messages, his actions, and his life experiences. This is the expedient way for you to understand Grace as a state of consciousness from which Grace-full blessings flow.

Within each one of these stages, (Mortal, Metaphysical, Mystic, Master, and Mind) the principles of Grace—abundance, acceptance, and freedom—can be *witnessed* within your consciousness as they are functioning from varying *degrees* of your understanding. As you begin to examine your application of the Grace teachings of Jesus, your understanding will expand, and you will be able to more easily identify what stage of the journey you are in at any given moment.

Christ knew Grace as a state of consciousness automatically flowing from the true nature of his Being. This true nature was the same nature of his Father, which was Jesus' Divine inheritance of Peace, Love, and Joy. Jesus emphasized all that the Father has was his, and all that was his is ours. He understood his inheritance of Peace to be the consciousness flowing from him in alignment with the infinite ideas of God that are already fulfilled. *"Peace I leave with you; my peace I give to you; not as the world gives do I give to you."* (John 14:27) He understood that the ideas that rested in their fulfillment were not of *this world* but of the world of Spirit. In the 20th chapter of *Gospel of John*, Jesus lets us know this same

Peace is within us. Three times he says, *"Peace be with you."*
(John 20: 19, 21, 26) His consciousness of *acceptance* of these
ideas was the environment that called them forth in his ministry
of miracles. His miracles all reflected an *abundance* of our true
inheritance—health, life, love, peace, joy, harmony, wisdom,
and similar qualities. His miracles manifested an abundance
of whatever was needed, such as food, wine, calm seas, and
parables for his message. They manifested instantly and
abundantly because Jesus understood the principle of abundance
functioning together with the principle of acceptance, which was
activated by his freewill choice functioning within the principle
of his innate freedom.

Jesus understood all Divine ideas were continually
seeking to manifest from their own true nature, which was
also abundance, acceptance, and freedom. All they needed
was a consciousness that would *freely accept* their *abundance.*
He knew his spiritual DNA of Love was the moving force of
acceptance that attracted all the Divine ideas within his Essence
of Peace. He understood God as the creative principle of infinite
ideas, and that we access these ideas every time we are stilled
in our own true nature of *peacefulness* (a Divine idea within
Peace). Jesus implied that Love was the moving force of the
Divine idea to love; he continually exemplified love in every
aspect of his life and encouraged us to do likewise: *"A new
commandment I give unto you, that you love one another; even
as I have loved you, that you also love one another. By this all
men will know that you are my disciples, if you have love for
one another."* (John 13:34) Would we not choose to be disciples
of Christ? Then we must, in every aspect of our lives, express
the infinite ideas of love beckoning to us from Peace, Love, and
Joy—the spiritual DNA of our Being.

Jesus lived, moved, and had his Being in a state of Joy, the
natural energy of consciousness as the synthesis of Peace and Love,
flowing *freely* through him. *"These things I have spoken to you,
that my joy may be in you, and that your joy may be full."* (John
15:11) Jesus walked the earth, fulfilled his mission, and performed
his miracles from this state. He encouraged us to express our true
nature of Joy which is independent of a need for reason.

Throughout Jesus' ministry he continually offered parables to exemplify his Essence as our own. These parables were reflective mirrors of life as related to the people and their relationship to God, self, and others. Following in the footsteps of Christ, we are going to enter now into a study that mirrors your Essence through your experiences and relationships. As you seek to become more fully awakened in Grace, you will find that the experience of life offers barometers by which to measure degrees of awakening. Without experience there is no point of reference from which to know exactly where you stand in your spiritual evolution. How will you ever know if you have mastered non-judgment unless you are given the opportunity not to judge? How will you know if you can love unconditionally unless you have the opportunity to apply the Love vibration to a situation or person in close proximity? How will you know you have conquered fear unless you are willing to face fear and see it for what it is?

I call this study, 'Mirrors of Grace.' Each mirror reflects different aspects of your spiritual DNA engaging the three principles or laws of Grace functioning in the creative process. At first you may see the faces of ego states as they present themselves from altered positions of your true nature. These faces are reflective of Mortal Mind. Look deeply into each mirror to find veiled understandings that will help you align your thinking with Grace consciousness or Master Mind awareness. The mirrors serve as reflectors that, ultimately, enable you to see the face of Christ with the single 'I.' They will also be of great assistance in recognizing the shift from one level of the spiritual journey of Grace awakening to another. As you look into each mirror, you will see the ego unmasked, revealing its face as simply the reflection of your limited understanding of your Divinity. Ultimately, Christ is the Essence of each mirror that enables you to see your own reflections. Christ is the loving Presence of yourself that accepts, without judgment, whatever is revealed.

The four mirrors addressed in the following pages are, in essence, one mirror reflecting deeper and deeper pools of inner vision. Clear insight into one enables clearer vision of the next. They are somewhat progressive in nature as is your spiritual awakening in Grace. Each one serves as an 'Open Sesame' to the kingdom within, so let us begin.

Mirror Number One

The Mirror of Your Relationships

Your magnetic field of attraction: like attracts like, and opposites attract

This is the mirror of your present *experience* of Reality. It reflects back to you, in equal measure, what you are outwardly or inwardly expressing and doing as the result of your own inner posture. Your actions are in direct alignment with your feelings, emotions, beliefs, and judgments, and your current experience of Reality is directly proportional to those inner and outer actions. Your current relationships will show you exactly how *you* are responding to life, to others, and ultimately to the focus of your inner world. The degree to which you have explored the depths of yourself will determine your ability to recognize your inner patterns that are reflected to you through another human being's behavior or your current situation. This mirror exemplifies the universal principle of "like attracts like" as well as "opposites attract." Your outer world always reflects your current inner positions—*abundantly,* since your inner positions are what have been *accepted*!

This is always the first mirror to be understood in the ascension process into Grace consciousness. It is the most difficult mirror to fully acknowledge and accept, for the ego is a master at projecting onto another something it doesn't like or refuses to acknowledge about itself. This is a classic position of Mortal Mind which sees everything 'out there' with no relationship to 'in here'—me. The aspirant will not be able to advance in the evolutionary spiral of awakening in Grace until this mirror is fully recognized and understood. Every other step depends upon it.

It is paramount that you take a full inventory of your motives, judgments, prejudices, fears, control issues, core beliefs, and areas of focused observation to determine the mirroring status in every relationship. This inventory is easily accessible through asking this question: *is there any face within me that mirrors the one or the situation that stands before me?* Revelation will be given to you in direct proportion to the purity of your heart's intention to know the truth about yourself.

When you find the same face in yourself that is facing you in the outer world, you must first *accept* that you are sending out an invitation from the level of the behavior reflected in that face. Do not try to resist what you find or to get rid of it, because resistance is a subtle level of acceptance and will multiply abundantly what you don't want in the outer. Become still and empty for the purpose of receiving assistance from Gracemind. Do not rationalize, analyze, or criticize. Do not go on a 'witch hunt' within yourself to find the cause. That is just not necessary and makes you a detective seeking a guilty party. No, no, no! If you are reading this book, you have already done enough of that. This practice has served its purpose of helping you realize a multitude of dysfunctional states of mind. In the past, what have you done with these causes when you found them? You attempted to heal them by getting rid of them. Has it worked? Grace heals from the Essence of its own nature. It really needs no assistance from you other than acceptance at the level of your Divinity—Peace, Love, and Joy. Accept the outpouring of these three—it is what Jesus did!

The law of *attraction* is always responding to the vibration of your energy, whether that is positive, negative, or true to the nature of your Being. It is that simple—it attracts, it multiplies, it increases, and manifests an equivalent in the world of form and experience. God's precious law of Grace always deals with increase—more, not less, and it is indifferent to *what* is increased. When you think about something or give your inner attention to it, you emit a vibration equal to the intensity of the thought, feeling, or action. The universe, which operates within the law of acceptance, then responds to your vibration, attracting whatever is the equivalent in expression of your predominant vibration. It's like a radio signal you are sending out. As you vibrationally output, consciously or unconsciously, the universe receives the signal from your point of awareness and matches it.

It makes no difference whether you are observing something, coming to a decision about something, believing in something, or remembering or imagining something; you are offering a vibrational output which will be attracted to a match.

What you desire most is to be a vibrational match with your Divine nature, or God Essence and the goodness that Essence promises in manifestation. It is rare to become a perfect vibrational match to this desire because contained within you is the memory or belief in something seemingly separate or in opposition to your Divinity. If you have been on a *conscious* spiritual path for some time, you may be well into the practice of positive thinking—aligning your vibrations with affirmations, thoughts of goodness, and good things that are the promises of the kingdom of God. You may affirm the abundance of money in the bank, harmonious relationships, a new car, or home. These are all Divine ideas resting within the consciousness of Peace as already fulfilled. They are reflective of an abundance of goodness. However, as soon as you drop the affirmations, you may find you are engulfed in fearful feelings of what it is like to experience lack in these areas. Your focus of energy identifies with what you don't want, and the universe, by the law of attraction, seeks to match that thought in manifestation. One vibration will either nullify another or attract the stronger in the outer.

In trying to eliminate the unwanted thing from your life, somewhere in your early experience you became convinced that you must push away what you do not want in order to make room for what you do want. The law of attraction says, the more you push, the more focused energy you give to the unwanted. The universe, which does not understand exclusion, only acceptance, seeks only to do what is true to its nature which is to bring that very thing to you. With this understanding, you can clearly see how you can desire one thing but draw to yourself the exact opposite due to the effect of any energy that is focused on elimination of the unwanted.

Often, awakening aspirants will begin to see faces of their parents reflecting back at them through their relationships. As they look deep within themselves, they will uncover unwanted elements of their own thinking and behavior that reflect their parents' dysfunctional behavior. If they try to push that away, they will only develop more of that same character trait, attracting more relationships that mirror their parents. I saw a plaque in a store recently that made me chuckle, for it expressed the truth of this mirror with humor. It said, "Mirror, mirror, on the wall, I've become my mother after all!"

A deeper focus into the principle of this first mirror reveals a paradoxical truth in some situations: "Opposites attract *because* like attracts like." Very often you will be fully focused on the *ideal* from every position within you. By 'position' I mean you are affirming the ideal, thinking about the ideal, emotionally excited about the ideal, feeling the ideal, and so on. Your thinking, feeling, and doing of something less than the ideal has become so faint it no longer carries enough energy to emit a vibration from you that attracts. For instance, you may have mastered patience. You are patient in every aspect of life, but as you look out into your life you become aware you have drawn impatient people into your surroundings. How can this be if like attracts like? Very simply stated, your new mindset of patience is attracting the nature of patience in others though that aspect may be masked by their sense of separation and collected fears. They are attracted by your Light because the Light within them is seeking to shine. They are not shining yet, but your Light is drawing it forth. Like is attracting like at the level of Spirit, and opposites are attracting in the process of fulfilling that design.

Many students at the level of Metaphysical Mind become confused or discouraged by this truth, but, when understood from the nature of Grace, it becomes the most exciting aspect of the law of attraction. If you are truly holding only the consciousness of Love within you, trust that if the universal law of Grace attracts a negative vibration into your life, it is being drawn to the more loving one to transmute it and bring it into the expanded awareness of Gracemind. This is the metaphysical understanding of how it was possible for Jesus to have attracted enemies. If the law of abundance was complete at the level of like attracts like, Christ could not have had enemies. The Light that was within Jesus was, unbeknown to his enemies, attracting their spiritual Light.

We see this aspect of Grace at work in relationships and events around the world in growing numbers, because the increased vibrational attunement of consciousness to Gracemind is drawing everything unlike itself to the surface. In a successful business, the top management positions are filled with people who have the greatest capacity to resolve conflict and bring resolution through their focus on harmony, love, and wisdom. Yet, they are the ones who are continually drawing fires into their offices to be put out. In greater numbers, children with traumatic cellular memory at the soul level are being drawn to parents with the greatest capacity of patience and unconditional love. This is happening in reverse as well. Children of very high vibrational energy are being born into low energy environments as catalysts for healing. Even Mother Earth is responding with upheaval and chaos as the consciousness of Love and Peace becomes more and more the collective consciousness of humanity. She is giving birth to a new earth as we bring down heaven from above, and everything unlike heaven that has been collected in the cellular memory of our beloved planet is being eliminated.

This mirror also reveals that what you admire the most in others is reflective of a soul quality you are seeking to have fully realized in yourself. Often, however, you will have a very strange reaction to people you draw into your life who express the qualities you most admire. This quality will sometimes turn you completely off. For example: let's say you are learning "truth needs no defense," and you truly admire another's ability to practice this. You may draw someone into your life who has mastered this soul quality and simply has no need to argue with you. Because your viewpoints are different, and because you haven't mastered defenselessness through acceptance, you will get angry because s/he won't argue back. Of course, the opposite may also happen. You may draw someone who, like you, is still very defensive. Like attracts like, but, remember, it is also true that opposites attract, because like attracts like. These examples are reflective of the two properties of the Grace-full principles of abundance and acceptance (laws of attraction) in soul development.

Mastery is not accomplished by focusing on your shortcomings. You have learned that to do this is to perpetuate them. Resistance to your shortcomings (such as fear and judgment, for example) only feeds their negative behavior patterns and attracts more of what is resisted. Your purpose and your true heart's desire is to embody and freely express those soul qualities inherent within you that are reflective of the true nature of Grace. To the extent you are bottled up in resistance will you be denying your true Self—your greatest gifts and your heart's desires.

It is important as you continue to stand before the focus of this mirror not to get discouraged or dismayed by what you see. Nor must you try to discern whether it is *your* inner posture or whether it is the inner posture of the one who stands before you that is askew. It matters not which of the two of you has manifested the undesirable. The only thing that is important is the re-membering of your vibration to Love in any given moment; this is what changes the face in the mirror and creates a new world for you and the one looking back at you. Thus, the grand design for the continual evolution of consciousness progresses by the miraculous law of Grace which always deals with the increase of Essence awareness through alignment to the vibration to Love.

The faces in the mirror of your relationships are deeply veiled and will begin to magnify as you approach the advanced stages of Metaphysical Mind. A clue of this advancement will be the realization that you have a charge (an emotional response) to *another's* behavior which you perceive is no longer present in yourself. Once you clean up patterns of your behavior that are the effects of deeply seeded error beliefs, you will most likely shift your pattern of response. You will shift from actually *expressing* or doing the behavior you don't like, to *seeing* in another the same negative behavior you think you have overcome in yourself. For example: let's say in looking closely at yourself you discovered that you were constantly being criticized because you actively focused on finding fault with others—even if your criticisms were not verbalized. This resulted in drawing into your life those who found fault with you and most of your efforts. You have prayed for this pattern of mind to be transformed so that you no longer have the need to do such an ungodly thing, and you have succeeded to a great degree. Now, however, your emotional buttons get pushed every time you see someone else criticizing. You pride yourself in no longer doing this, and it really gets to you when others do. You may think you have overcome being critical, but the pattern of mind has simply shifted its position of criticism. Now you are critical of others who criticize. Your thoughts and feelings are realigned with your old way of thinking, and you find yourself still attracting people who criticize you and others. This seemingly elevated position of mind does not immunize you from the law of attraction. Examine your charges and you will understand why you are attracting the same experiences which mirror your old mental practices.

It is important to remember that the subconscious is the storehouse of all thoughts, feelings, and emotions. It cannot make distinctions. It simply records the feelings and the emotions, and through the law of attraction/acceptance the vibrational frequency of the emotion will draw into your life what you have deemed acceptable or unacceptable for self or another.

Aspirants will often approach this reflective mirror with the question: "What is it in my consciousness that is drawing this to me?" In the frantic search, they can't find anything that resembles the behavior that is showing up. This is the time to look deeper to see if you have any judgmental emotion that has been elevated to the level of a charge. If you do not acknowledge this, you will remain in a sense of victimization, unable to become 'karma-cly' free of the reflection of your charge. When all else fails, examine what appear to be your virtues.

Many aspirants have big issues regarding control and freedom. Are you one of them? Your need to control is the ego's way of making you think you are protected from other controlling people. The egoic logic of Mortal Mind surmises that you have to control first in order to not be controlled. You are out to protect your freedom at all costs. The only thing this really accomplishes is the generation of more controlling people and circumstances in your life. Like attracts like. For years you have worked on releasing your need to control, knowing this will free you and the ones you are trying to control. You have really done a pretty good job. You pride yourself in giving your children your support as they make their choices in life. You feel very good about no longer needing to have others believe exactly as you do. If you don't get your way about something, you don't go bananas any more. Good for you. You've made wonderful progress, but what transpires within your soul when someone tries to control you or someone you love? How do you feel about controlling people? I'll bet you're pretty good at spotting manipulators, aren't you? Uh Huh! Because you have not freed yourself from or made peace with the need to pass judgment on those who control, you will continue to draw controlling people and situations into your life. Gracemind understands God is the only control. *Accept* this truth and you will not feel your buttons pushed in relation to control issues—your own or another person's.

This is a very subtle movement of mind and must be closely monitored in order to detect. The ego will jump to the front lines with the illusionary reasoning that you are most justified in your judgment, and that this judgment will somehow correct *their* error behavior or impulse you into an action that will. Think again! The great cosmic law of Grace reveals you cannot solve the problem on the level of the problem—you must rise above it. You always perpetuate the problem by the intensity of your energy in resistance to it. Your vibration of resistance from this position is a perfect match to the very thing you desire to eliminate.

At some point during the course of the eternal journey you will be required to relinquish *all* judgment. This is the most difficult hurdle for Mortal Mind and Metaphysical Mind to surmount. In your sense of separation, judgment has motivated your patterns of behavior that have kept you in a false sense of protection. Judgment is a survival mechanism of the ego.

It is important to note there is a big difference between judgment and discernment. Judgment releases negative degenerative energy vibrations that are harmful and destructive. Discernment is the quality of God that impulses Divine action. When the ego is no longer in charge, discernment will flow freely and abundantly through your soul with its purest intention and impulse you to Divine action.

To assist you in uncovering your charges, I offer this simple exercise to pinpoint where you are leaking judgmental energy. Ask yourself what it is that you pride yourself in the most. The opposite of that soul quality, when expressed by others, will usually trigger your charge issues. For example, are you giving? If so, how do you feel about stingy, tight people? Are you open-minded? How do you feel about narrow-minded people? Do you always give people the benefit of the doubt? Then is it hard for you to deal with people who look for the worst in others? What do you feel when someone tries to proselytize you? You respect others' privacy and space. You wouldn't do that, but does your button get pushed when you receive unsolicited telephone calls? Are you a courteous driver? Sure. What goes through your mind when you encounter bullies on the road? Do you respond with *road rage* or unconditional love?

Truthful responses to what you pride yourself in the most and how you feel about others who do not exhibit the same quality will be well worth while in facilitating understanding of yourself. The mystery as to why you still keep drawing certain experiences and relationships into your life may be uncovered. Your emotional charges will keep you suspended in the abyss of social consciousness and forever tied to the bucking horse.

Over time, as you make a practice of looking into this mirror, very subtle shifts will begin to take place within. You will slowly be able to see, with clarity, what you see in another *is* in yourself. You will begin to glimpse little fragments of de-ja-*you*!

Mirror Number Two

The Mirror of Your Yearning

That which you feel has been lost, destroyed,
taken away, or you never had

We have already talked a good deal about yearning, but it is important to realize that when you don't understand the true nature of desire, your yearning may be reflecting deep-rooted content of mind that continues to make choices in the creative process from a vibrational focus of despair. Yearning, at the level of Mortal Mind, is a longing for what you perceive you do not have and cannot get. If you could instantly awaken to the truth, you would see you could have everything you possibly desire if you were in harmony with your true nature. Until that moment occurs, you will draw relationships and situations into your life that reflect back to you the seemingly unattainable fulfillment or the absence of what you most want. The reason for this is that beneath your yearning for what you desire lies the hidden assumption, 'I don't have access to what I want.'

The opposite spectrum of yearning for what you don't have is the fear you may lose, have stolen, or have taken away what you do have. The mind which desires from the vibrational belief that it does not have what it wants attracts *more,* not less, of what it doesn't want. Universal law is oblivious to *what* is attracted. It never produces less of anything. Remember, consciousness does not understand exclusion; it only understands inclusion. God is all inclusive, not exclusive. This is why what you resist persists, and why what you try to eliminate from your life increases.

Look closely again at all your yearnings, and you will find many of them may be anchored in a fear of *lack, or loss.* All fears are based on these perceptions when taken to their core, even the universal ones such as the fear of abandonment or separation, the fear of death, the fear of being unworthy, the fear of not enough, and the fear of disease. Abandonment and separation imply *exclusion*; fear of death implies *absence* of life; not feeling worthy implies not being good enough; fear of disease implies *absence* of ease and *lack* of health. Therefore, as you allow yourself to focus clearly on all your desires, you will uncover your most deeply hidden *fears of lack or loss.* But remember, *God, functioning in the universe, does not recognize loss or lack. God only knows increase—more!* This makes all your fears unfounded as well as out of vibrational harmony with *more* of the very thing for which you yearn.

Be willing to look more deeply into yourself now by examining your desires to see where you have pushed the very thing you want away from you, or attracted into your life in someone else the very thing you feel you no longer have, want to have, or are afraid of losing. This is the magnetic field of attraction that most new relationships are founded upon. Each individual sees in the other individual what s/he thinks s/he lost, had taken away, gave away, or never had.

I know a young man who met a woman and immediately got in touch with what it was about her that attracted him. It was her sense of innocence. Later he found himself weeping as he touched that spot in his soul memory that felt as though he had *lost* his sense of innocence due to his drive to *figure everything out.*

In a recent workshop a couple shared with me that, when they met, the man was immediately attracted to his partner's playfulness and child-like spontaneity, while the woman was attracted to his depth of wisdom and maturity. Both felt each was reflecting something he or she did not have! The man grew up in a very strict household where hard work and no play were the norm. The woman, in childhood, was never validated for her wisdom and cleverness. In both, the relationship grew into deep love for one another for the first year. At the end of the first year, or honeymoon period, the deep sense of lack each felt buried deeply beneath their admiration turned into anger and resentment toward the other person. Their sense of lack within themselves came to the surface, creating conflict and dissatisfaction in the relationship. They did not begin to heal until both realized they were perfect mirrors for the other's beliefs. They healed by *embracing the true nature* in their partner which called forth that same nature within them.

She found a variety of ways to invite his inner child to come out and play through spontaneity instead of structure. She would lure him to the children's park to play on the swings, creating an environment where it was safe for him to express childlike playfulness. They would become children again by going to the local fair, eating cotton candy, enjoying the scary rides, and laughing at themselves in the hall of mirrors. They would dress up on Halloween and go out with the kids of the neighborhood. They drew pictures, made treasure maps of their dreams, played checkers and scrabble. They once even bought coloring books and took them on a picnic. They took nature walks, rolled down hills, and blew bubbles in the wind.

He made a conscious effort to find new ways of helping her to see her own inner wisdom; often he would look into her eyes and tell her of the intelligence he saw there, reinforcing to her it was one of the qualities he recognized and appreciated. He began to express how deeply he loved the depth of her mind—one of the qualities that had attracted him to her in the first place. She loved the study of metaphysics, which had been his lifelong passion. He told her how wonderful it was to have someone to dialogue with in this field of study. She had a rare eye for beauty and a flare for interior decorating; he was quick to acknowledge the genius of her creativity. He recognized when she was reacting to feelings of being incompetent or stupid, and he would hold her close, softly reminding her that those feelings were nothing more than the scar tissue of childhood experiences.

You can never give away, lose, have taken away, or be anything less than what is true of the nature of God, for you are created in God's image and likeness. You can only increase what is attracted to you by what you accept. *"With our unveiled faces reflecting like mirrors the brightness of the Lord, all grow brighter as we are turned into the image that we reflect."* (2 Cor. 3:18)

To help clear the focus of this mirror, take a reality check in your mind of your heart's yearnings. Make a list of them. Grab a sheet of paper or your journal and simply begin listing things you desire. Your list of items will most likely fit into one of these categories: (1) material objects; (2) a soul quality aspiration; (3) healing of a mental, emotional, or physical condition; (4) change in relationships; (5) spiritual expansion; and/or (6) a life achievement.

Beside each desire, identify which of these categories your desire seems to fit. Does the item reflect something you feel you have never had, have lost, have given away, or had taken from you? Now, see if you can make a correlation to help you identify your fears of loss. Then see them for the illusions they are, thus opening your mind and heart to a tremendous shift. Instead of seeing desire as *yearning for something you do not have, see it as the impulse from your Divine Essence to accept what is already and always has been yours.*

Once you have identified your desires, the category each fits into, the core belief, and the core fear, you will begin to see *why* some of your desires elude you. They rest in a deep rooted belief that generates an emotion of fear at the subjective level of consciousness.

We are constantly looking to our relationships and outer situations to fill the empty space this type of yearning creates. They can never do this for us, and this is why we are always disappointed in people and events that don't provide for us what we think we desire. This causes us to project our judgment onto another person and feel deeply frustrated when they don't give us what we think we need.

Mirror Number Three

The Mirror of Your Fear

Your most forgotten truth

As you learned in the previous mirror, fears are not in vibrational harmony with your Source or your true nature. The law of attraction does not distinguish between fears and desires. The only way to break the cycle and free yourself from the consequences of your fears is to face them and see them for what they are—illusions, masking from you forgotten truths and your greatest potential gifts. It is essential to recognize that your previous methods of confrontation with your core fears have been somewhat ineffective.

For example, as a child you may have experienced the repeated anger or even rage a parent directed at you, which you associated with rejection. You may have interpreted the behavior as an indication that you were not 'worthy' or 'good enough.' Over time, you developed ways to avoid confrontations and rejections, such as not expressing your real feelings, not voicing your opinions, throwing little temper tantrums, or going into hiding whenever the feelings started to surface. You probably developed an early warning system to alert you to the potential onset of the behavior to be avoided—typically a feeling of tenseness in the pit of the stomach or solar plexus.

Learned behavioral patterns of childhood and adolescence usually carry over into adulthood. Using the previous example, as an adult you may continue to avoid expressing your true feelings and/or get very tense whenever the feeling arises or when you sense the onset of some act of rejection. Any expressed anger by another is immediately registered as threatening and as rejection of you. Ironically, for those in relationship with you, your protective behavior is often viewed by them as withdrawal, aloofness, indifference, or even rejection on your part toward them. It may even draw anger from the other person, thereby re-affirming to you the validity of your insecurity. In other words, the behavioral patterns developed early in your life unintentionally draw to you the very thing you seek to escape. These patterns seem to have a life of their own, leaving you feeling hopeless and helpless.

The truth is, you are and always have been worthy. While you may have been the recipient or seeming victim of the expressed anger of another, the source of the anger was within the other person. Although you perceived yourself as being rejected, in actuality it was some activity you did or failed to do that triggered in the other person a feeling that *they* were powerless, not respected, not loved, or some other negative attribute. Whatever may have triggered it and however disguised, anger is an emotional response to a perceived threat and a call for love. If the anger is recognized for what it truly is, it can be responded to with acceptance rather than with resistance, thereby disarming the one feeling threatened and making it safe for both parties to break the behavioral pattern.

Unfortunately, those on the receiving end of anger or disgust tend to see it as a form of rejection or attack, rather than for what it really is, causing them to go into a protective and often emotional state of resistance to the behavior. The resistance feeds the fear of the other person, and the mirroring effect kicks in, intensifying and amplifying the fears and emotions of both parties. This can result in one or both parties feeling emotionally injured, thereby reinforcing the fears and further fueling the habitual, debilitating process. This feeding frenzy continues until one or the other can break the cycle.

The pain you experience is directly proportional to the degree of your unwillingness to face your fears or to resolve them by remembering the truth. The habitual behavior developed to protect yourself from the pain of these 'Friday Night Fright Shows' pushes you ever deeper into your illusions and further from your forgotten truth.

Innumerable examples can be given of these cycles of degenerative behavior which arise from unfounded, seemingly justified, or illusory fears. They become your *story*, and it is important to recognize that your core fears are the fuel that sustain ego. In addition to unnatural behavior patterns, core fears perpetuate disharmony, disease, lack, judgmental thoughts, accidents, and all addictions. In order to face your particular fears and recognize what they are mirroring, it is helpful to identify what is at the core of all fear—nothing!

At the core of all fear is the mirror that reflects *nothing*. This nothing represents the *unknown*. Within the unknown there is no point of reference upon which to place your identity, thus your identity feels threatened. Ironically, at the core of all life is the impulse to embrace more life, or more of the unknown. Such is the nature of consciousness because it is ever expanding in awareness. Can you accept the fact that every fear has its root in this truth? If so, then simply become nonresistant to the fear, and *embrace it as a call to a greater truth that rests in Essence.*

Consciousness awakening to the unknown feels very threatened when it cannot see beyond the current point of reference, so you feel fearful. This awareness mirrors the beginning stages of the Mystic Mind which is obsessed with unveiling the fears of illusion, surrendering them to the Divine for transformation, and diving deeper into unexplored territory of Mind.

In the process of becoming more expanded in awareness, consciousness is drawn in upon itself in pursuit of a greater knowingness. As it does this, it brings along with it the collective understanding it has gathered through many evolutions in life. In order to expand the seeming boundaries of your boundless Self, you are asked, by the impulse of Love, to be willing to leave behind the bundles of content you consider to be the known. You are being asked to explore the infinite kingdom of God consciousness that is your Divine inheritance.

To the ego, this looks like an invitation to embark into unknown worlds and unfamiliar territory which may cause it to completely lose its identity. The ego's fear is justified. The truth of the matter is this territory represents the familiar womb of God from which you emerged. You have been and always will be one with the unknown, the infinite Mind that sets you free to be more of what you are created to be.

In the beginning, you existed in a state of consciousness that knew but didn't know it knew. So, in a very real sense, your awakening can be likened to waking up from the amnesia of eternal life. You are remembering what you knew in the beginning, but now you are remembering with the additional awareness of knowing that you know. Each fear then will masquerade some glorious truth you have, in Essence, forgotten.

You don't really fear the unknown at all, but rather, the illusory perception your fear represents. Fears are the effect of some memory or belief that triggers an awareness of the possibility of loss or lack, which has its roots in the fear of annihilation, which can trace *its* roots to the fear of the unknown. Your fears are the overlays the ego has placed upon the soul in its journey of remembering. They are not based on any eternal principle of truth, for within them there is no truth. They are perceptions as content of consciousness you have gathered in your efforts to awaken in a polarized existence. In other words, they are the effects of judgments you have placed upon what you have manifested in awakening to your creative potential; a harvesting of the fruits of good and evil, plucked from the Tree of the Knowledge of Good and Evil. Our wisdom texts tell us this has been a good thing and is as it should be, but the greater scriptural promise is you are destined to awaken to and partake of the Tree of Life in which there is no good or evil—there is just Life! You are asked to transcend the consciousness of duality while still existing in a polarized world. This is not an easy task and can only be done when there is a willingness to be cleansed of all perceptions that show their faces of fear.

The process of healing through the pathway of your forgotten truth must begin with identifying your protective behavioral patterns of fear. Simply ask yourself: what are my reactions every time I feel _____? (name the uncomfortable feeling and describe your reactions); to what fear could these behavior patters be related?; how do I camouflage my fear? Now, turn within and go deep into your Essence and ask: what is the eternal truth hidden by this fear?

As noted, your pattern of behavior becomes habitual, making you feel so removed from your fear you may not even recognize it. It is essential to become conscious of any emotion or feeling that is less than peace, love, or joy, for this awareness provides the opportunity for you to remember your most forgotten truth and to free yourself from deeply rooted misperceptions. This is the real process of spiritual evolution. To the degree you are free, happy, and functioning *from* Love, are you advancing on your spiritual path. Staying locked into fear patterns is stagnation at its best and degeneration at its worst.

Once you have identified your key behavioral patterns around fear, you should be able to pinpoint the core fears from which you are seeking to escape. Each core fear is a mirror of a forgotten truth you are being asked to remember. The key is to not dwell upon or seek to overcome the illusory fear, but rather to simply observe it, watch yourself, allow it to express, and then *identify with the truth it veils*—you are the *eternal life* of the unknown, knowing itself!

When truth is remembered at the conscious level, it establishes a vibratory resonance field that serves as a magnetic attractor of the eternal truth that is at all times resting within Gracemind. Once again the law of attraction is at work. When all of consciousness is in resonance, this harmony nullifies everything unlike itself and transforms it into a state of Grace. In this way, all that is contained as subconscious memory which is not in alignment with Essence becomes exposed by the light of truth and becomes the truth known. As you advance in the healing process, you will become less and less enamored with identifying your fears and more adamant in identifying truth. This is the way of healing by Grace. But the process of identifying your fears is very enlightening when it comes to understanding the creative process and realizing why your life is the way it is. Continue to identify your fears, and then turn them over to healing through Grace until Gracemind overtakes you, and that process is no longer necessary. Take your fear and place it into the heart of the Grace Prayer (see chapter seven). It is magical.

The more you engage the principles of Grace, any memories that are not the truth of your Being may never be revealed to you but simply transmuted or alchemized by the Gracemind vibrations of Love. This is the journey of the mystic and can be a long one if it is approached with any resistance.

Mirror Number Four

The Mirror of Your Essence

Your gifts revealed

This mirror underlies the previous mirror, waiting to be revealed through the resolution of your fears and your willingness to leap into unknown territory beyond the reasoning mind. It fully reveals itself on the other side of surrender and is the effect of complete acceptance of the unknown. This mirror ultimately reflects Master Mind/Gracemind awareness as it radiates your true nature, your individualized expression of that nature, and the nature of Reality. As you have seen, your behavior patterns often mask your core fears, which, in turn, veil your most forgotten truths. Your most forgotten truths unlock any resistance to your Essence. Once living from Essence, your mission, gifts, talents, and creativity express effortlessly, and door after door opens for the opportunity of those expressions. You do not have to wait for Essence to fully awaken before gazing into this mirror to recognize its treasures. Your coded destiny has been impulsing your gifts and talents from the beginning. Looking at what you love to do and what comes naturally to you are the faces this mirror reveals and will speed your awakening.

Your individuated gifts and talents glorify God when expressed through you freely. No other person has your exact coding. Each person is a vital, unique contribution to the whole for the glorification of God. How do you access this mirror even before it becomes completely clear? By doing what brings you the most joy in every single moment of your life. In that doing, you will feel the Peace, Love, and Joy of your eternal soul bringing every aspect of your consciousness to a resonating field equal to your Divine nature. This is the way of awakening by Grace.

Any time you find yourself not engaged in what you love to do, your awareness of Peace, Love, and Joy will elude you. This is always a clue that you need to reactivate or make a change that will empower you to spend more time gazing into this mirror's reflection. As a matter of fact, identifying your gifts and giving more and more of yourself to their expression quantums your awakening into Master Mind consciousness as the fully awakened state of Grace.

As Essence is revealed and lived from your consciousness, you will begin to experience higher and higher frequencies of energy that draw you into creative endeavors that call forth expanded expressions of your original design. Your gifts and talents are enhancers that add brilliance, polish, and shine to your current mission and world service. The more you identify with them, the more their frequency will be integrated into every aspect of your awareness, your soul, your body, and all activities. If you will gaze into this mirror as much (or more) than you do the previous ones and put into practice what is revealed, you will find Grace awakening to be a glorious experience. You will be awakening through creativity, doing what you love to do best. This practice activates the highest vibrational frequencies of consciousness that match Essence, elevating lesser frequencies into higher ones. The more you participate in doing what you love, the more the law of attraction serves to transform illusions and awaken spiritual gifts. Doing what you love cannot be emphasized enough as a tool for accelerated spiritual advancement. This practice will always lead you into the fullness of your mission and purpose for this incarnation.

Obviously, there are certain things in life you must do that you are not ecstatic about doing in order to survive, maintain order, respect policies and social moirés, get certain tasks and goals accomplished, etc. **Don't hear me say not to do these things!** Do hear me say not to do them from a space of distaste, anger, resentment, martyrdom, or resistance of any kind. Find a way to ***bring the love you are*** into the doing even though you may not love ***what*** you are doing. By now you know the consequences if you don't.

This mirror also offers you an opportunity to see and appreciate the gifts, talents, and missions of others. Appreciation registers in you first, expanding your capacity to recognize and feel your own gifts related to the whole. As you look outward, practice seeing others' gifts and how they weave themselves into a glorious tapestry of exquisite beauty, glorifying God. Look for the not so obvious ones: a mother's gift of bringing peace and a sense of safety with just a touch, a look, or a kiss; a father's gift of approval bestowed upon his children that swaps a tear for a smile; the green thumb of the gardener that reveals itself as profuse blooms of nature's receptivity to silent love; the gift of spontaneous humor that breaks the ice or dispels the grip of fear; the offering of peace in the midst of chaos that restores order and harmony; the magic in someone's voice to make a story come alive in the telling; the gift of art presented by the chef; the gift of dance expressed in a puppy's love; the gift of wisdom found in a poet's verse; the healing balm of open arms extending hugs— *"seek, and ye shall find!"*

The more you focus on this mirror, the less you will feel the need to focus on the previous mirrors, for your gifts and talents, your mission and service, and your true spiritual Essence will become more and more awakened in you. Creativity releases a high frequency of Light from the level of your Divinity. That frequency becomes your focus and draws the totality of your awareness to its level. So, Beloved, do what you love and love in what you do. This is your destiny—the way to love the Lord *your* God with all your heart, soul and mind—the way of Grace.

Chapter Five

The Understanding

Chapter 5

The Understanding

Once you have examined the mirrors of your life and found some reflections of wrinkles and old baggage, it is time for a makeover. Makeovers always begin with the desire to see things differently. All the mirrors previously examined reflect both illusory content and truth of Being or Essence. Your goal now is to transform all content that no longer serves your beauty. Illusory content in the human soul is simply the reflection of frowns gathered in time from the frowns you have offered life. The good news is they can be exchanged for laugh lines once you understand the nature of their obsession.

Frowns are always expressed in the face of one who either disapproves or does not understand. These are two positions of brain mind that do not align with the true nature of Essence. They give birth to error beliefs. They make you feel sick at heart, lost, hopeless, angry, resentful, and cocooned—isolated in a sense of separation from God. They show up as judgments (effects of disapproval) and ignorance of understanding. When either of these energies is present, you undergo rapid aging through the degeneration of cells. All illusory content stems from these two positions. They are the forbidden fruit of the Garden of Eden, sweet Earth.

As you walk in the garden of your soul, you will see your belief systems as either the flowers you wish would flourish or the weeds that are choking them out. Your weeding will not be accomplished in the old way of hand to weed, one at a time; this is the antiquated method of applying the law of cause and effect. Instead, apply the fulfillment of the law, Gracemind. Watch, as it does the weeding from the outpouring of its Essence upon the garden, eliminating *all* the weeds in its path, as if by magic. This is the true way of transformation. It is the first and most paramount understanding that needs to be accepted by you who are ready to live *from* Grace.

Functions of Gracemind

Superconscious
Subconscious
Conscious

"Chalice of the Heart" by Lyrea Crawford

We will begin by examining the functions of consciousness that comprise Gracemind awareness. I like to think of these as stations of Mind. They are identified and categorized as the conscious, subconscious, and superconscious. A study of their true function will greatly enhance your understanding of Gracemind at work in the creative process. Do not confuse conscious, subconscious, and superconscious with my definitions of Mortal Mind, Metaphysical Mind, Mystic Mind, Master Mind, and Mind awakening in the spiritual journey. *The latter is descriptive of the mind's perceptions of awareness as Gracemind awakens in Essence.* Conscious, subconscious, and superconscious describe the stations of Mind as they were created to *operate or function* from awareness focused in Grace. Once you understand their true design, you will be able to synthesize the healing process as it takes place in Mind.

The chart on the next page is an attempt to integrate the stages of the spiritual journey with the awareness of the true functions of the conscious, subconscious and superconscious activities of Mind.

Your understanding, right now, of how the stations of Mind were created to function may be a bit veiled and resting in somewhat of an upside down position. Once they are fully understood and aligned, the pathways of awakening through Mortal, Metaphysical, Mystical, and Master Mind awareness

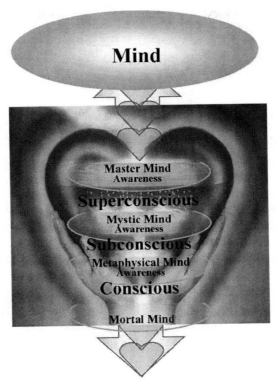

will integrate more fully and accelerate Grace awakening. This will sever the single thread that binds you to your illusions. You will then be drawn by Mind into a new creature in Christ—the butterfly set free.

Charles Fillmore, one of the co-founders of the Unity movement, was very inspirational in my understanding of the functions of Mind. He was one of the early mystics of our time who left a legacy of wisdom and love for us to absorb. The first time I read these passages from his book, *Keep A True Lent*, it was as if the windows of heaven had opened, pouring out many of the missing pieces of the cosmic puzzle. It would be many years later before I fully realized the depth of these words of wisdom. He writes:

The subconscious mind is the vast, silent realm that lies back of the conscious mind and between it and the superconscious... The subconscious may be called the sensitive plate of mind. Its true office is to receive impressions from the superconscious and to reproduce them upon the canvas of the conscious mind... Man, however, having lost the consciousness of the indwelling Father as an ever present reality, has reversed the process and impresses the subconscious from the conscious mind. Charles Fillmore, *KTL*, p. 87 – 88

The superconscious mind lifts up, or regenerates, both the subconscious and the conscious, transforming them into the true image and likeness of God. The conscious mind must be faithful during this transformation. It must look ever to the superconscious for all direction and instruction. It can of itself do nothing with assurance, because the Spirit of wisdom rests in the superconscious. Charles Fillmore, *KTL*, p. 89

The regeneration of the subconscious is not the work of the conscious, but of the superconscious mind acting in harmony with the conscious. Charles Fillmore, *KTL*, p. 91

Permission to reprint granted by Unity House, 1901 NW Blue Parkway, Unity Village, MO 64065

Once you are able to accept the fact that much of your life's experiences can be traced to the karmic wheel of the patterns spinning as thoughts, feelings, emotions, and belief systems in your mind, you immediately seek to stop them, reverse them, and change them. This sounds like a simple task when you first hear it. "Just stop thinking, feeling, or acting from your content," the teacher of wisdom instructs you. Well, try it—you won't like it. No matter how deeply you are committed to exchanging a positive for a negative or even better, bringing your mental processes to a halt through prayer, meditation, or affirmations— no deal. Your mind has a natural propensity for motion that will not take orders. Have you noticed?

The sincere metaphysical student embarks on an inner search into the ghettos of consciousness to find the garbage that needs to be cleaned up. I use the analogy of the trash compactor to get a good visual of the debris collected within the subconscious. How many pieces of trash have accumulated there, piece by piece, lifetime after lifetime—pressed down, shaken together, running over, and finally pouring into your lap? If you don't clean out your garbage on a regular basis, it just gets compacted, becoming heavier and heavier until it finally releases a toxic, poisonous gas. In your sincere desire to clean up the garbage of your subconscious, you often resort to bulimic action, trying to regurgitate all the content that has been swallowed.

The usual trial and error method that is applied as the source of removal is to locate the garbage piece by piece, wrap it in a sweet smelling affirmation, and then hope it will disappear. Affirmations are generated from the conscious mind which, in the upside down position of its true function, thinks it is in charge and can do the healing work. Affirmations are powerful tools for assisting the shifting of content from negative to positive ideas, but they can't do the depth of the healing work that is needed when it comes to lifetimes of accumulated concepts, beliefs, feelings, emotions, and memories that are not in harmonic resonance with original design. These memoirs are etched in cellular soul memory, and the only thing that works is new wine in new wine skins. Affirmations are conditioners that soften frizzed hair balls, but once the aspirant neglects to constantly use the conditioner, the hair ball returns in all its glory.

In your sincere efforts to heal soul memory, you may embark on a self induced investigation that doesn't work either. In the words of Charles Fillmore, *"The regeneration of the subconscious is not the work of the conscious, but of the superconscious mind acting in harmony with the conscious."* Christ reminds us: *"... I, when I am lifted up from the earth, will draw all men* (conditions, etc.) *to myself."* (John. 12:32)

The 'I' Jesus speaks of here is not his human, conscious mind but the superconscious/Gracemind that is of the Father. Christ knew the conscious mind was never created to heal or change anything. Its true function is to *"... look ever to the superconscious* (the Father) *for all direction and instruction. It can of itself do nothing with assurance, because the Spirit of wisdom rests in the superconscious."* (Fillmore) In the words of Jesus, *"... the Father who dwells in me does his works."* (John 14:10). When the conscious looks ever to the superconscious, the superconscious pours new wine into the subconscious and conscious, *transforming all their content*—not piece by piece but *Peace* by *Peace.*

Self analysis saves you from drowning or being swallowed up in the effects of your mental content, but like learning to swim, which is a good thing, you need not swim the entire depth and breadth of the Atlantic Ocean just because you have learned how to swim. It is not necessary to analyze the entire ocean of consciousness to become Graceminded. For Gracemind *is* the ocean of consciousness and knows the entire content of mind. If you are constantly diving into the deep waters of the subconscious you will exhaust yourself trying to analyze all that you find. Let the treasures of the ocean deep rise to the surface by way of focused surrender to the deeper levels of Mind where the Christ abides. Healing was meant to be a cruise in the journeying, not an ocean dredge churning up all the content of the waters. Carl Jung claimed the purpose of life was to make the subconscious conscious. That is true up to a point, but the greater truth is, the purpose of life is to make the superconscious conscious.

Beloved, it's just that simple, yet somehow it has turned into something complicated. This new understanding takes all the effort out of the healing process and cancels any dredging of consciousness one may be pursuing. This is the true meaning of the mystical vision received by the author of *The Book of Revelation:*

> *Behold, the dwelling of God is with men. He will dwell with them, and... he will wipe away every tear from their eyes, and death shall be no more, neither shall there be mourning nor crying nor pain any more, for*

the former things have passed away. And he who sat
upon the throne said, "Behold, I make all things new."
Rev. 21: 3-5

The subconscious can be viewed as the "sensitive plate" of mind that receives all impressions from both the conscious and the superconscious. It is a storehouse of all thoughts, feelings, beliefs, and memories conjured up from the conscious. It is also the storehouse of pure thought which is continually being resourced from the superconscious. The subconscious is fed from the Source of truth, eternal and endless, and also from the source of perception which is transient, temporal, and subject to fantasy. The subconscious is absent the capacity for 'choice.' It accepts all thoughts, feelings, and emotions at the level of their vibration, which in turn becomes the attracting frequency of a match in this world. The subconscious has no ability to discern positive from negative or a thought about self vs. another. It is simply the memory bank or holding tank of content. These factors will be important to remember as you deepen your understanding of the mental, emotional, and physical healing process.

The conscious is pivotal, gifted with the capacity to look inward to superconscious or outward to the world. If the subconscious has many lifetimes of stored collected memory as the result of the conscious pivoting outward to the world for love, wisdom, and understanding, it will more than likely perceive reality as duality, separation, and conflict. When there is a surplus of content absorbed in the impressionable subconscious from the conscious, it forms a dam of opposition between it and the superconscious. In the mystical stages of my own healing process, I came to identify this dam as the Wailing Wall.

This surplus also explains the traffic jam encountered when one first begins to try to reverse the process of the position of the conscious by looking inward through prayer and meditation to find its Source. It gets stuck in traffic for hours, going nowhere. If the aspirant is not diligent, patient, and non-judgmental of the practice, s/he may get discouraged and abandon the spiritual search, attempting to drop out of a required segment of the journey. This will only delay the inevitable.

A heart full of gratitude goes to Charles Fillmore for these insights into the functions of consciousness. I wonder if at the time he wrote them he realized what an impact they would eventually have upon the world, or if he knew the myriad pathways this wisdom would reveal to take us through our spiritual journey.

Here are a few insights that automatically occur as a result of understanding the correct positions of consciousness: (1) it alphabetizes your prayer life, putting it in right order from A to Z; (2) it places responsibility for change and healing where it belongs—in the hands of Gracemind, the superconscious; (3) it eliminates the struggle, the toiling, and the spinning of the mind; (4) it helps you become non-attached as you simply witness the healing instead of getting tangled up in it; (5) it strengthens your capacity to live in faith, trust, Peace, Love, and Joy during the transformative process; and (6) it reveals new methods of practicing the Presence.

As you dive deeper into the essence of the truth offered here by Charles Fillmore, and as you seek to fully awaken to the correct functioning of your Mind, you hasten the baptism of the Holy Spirit. Acceptance of the original design of consciousness becomes the invitation to the dove of Peace to begin its descent into awareness, setting things aright, and healing any content held in the subconscious that does not mirror Essence. This is the purpose of baptism; it is a perfect metaphor. Let's examine that process now in order to fully recognize it, accept it, and be changed by it in the twinkling of an eye.

Holy Spirit Regeneration ~ The Baptism

John the Baptist baptizes with water for repentance sake. Remember, repentance means to change your ways. The Gospel of John reports John the Baptist as saying: *"He on whom you see the Spirit descend and remain, this is he who baptizes with the Holy Spirit."* (John 1:33) He, Jesus, comes after John the

Baptist—after you have the pure heart intention to change your ways, perceptions, content of mind, and your mind's reversed order of functioning. Note: there is no mention of the word 'fire' associated with baptism by the Christ in *The Gospel According to John*. The three other Gospels all reference 'fire' in connection with baptism by the Christ. They report he will baptize with fire and the Holy Spirit. John does not claim this as a dynamic duo. Again, this implies that your metamorphosis was never meant to be painful. It was designed to be by way of the Christ which is full of Grace and truth. Remember my assignment? "You are here to help My children *'accept'* My Grace. Use *The Book of Love.*" Accept it, Beloved. Throw the erroneous concept of *no pain, no gain* out the window!

There was a wonderful book written by E.R.A. Crichton titled *No Mutiny From the Bounty, Your Miracle of Grace*. It was a book about the healing power of Grace absent any pain or suffering, trials, tribulation, or testing as its methods. That book is no longer in print, but its title alone is worth mentioning as a focus for meditation. No mutiny from the bounty of God's Grace is the journey of awakening as it was originally designed to be experienced.

"Grace gives God, not hardship. Struggle is not the way to realization of God, since in Him there is no contending. Crying is not the high road to laughter. Sometimes the cry must cease before the laugh begins. Light does not by battle banish the darkness. More than that, can light be aware of darkness? If, according to Saint John (1:5 of his Gospel), 'the light shineth in the darkness; and the darkness apprehended it not,' surely the light apprehendeth not the darkness."

Crichton, E.R.A. 1981. *No Mutiny from the Bounty*, p. 106. New York: Poise Publications.

The Second Coming

Jesus came to introduce a new way of living, believing, and relating to God. It is the way of intimacy, absent of fear. He came to introduce us to the Holy Spirit within that would teach us all things. He never indicated these teachings would be accompanied with pain and suffering. He came to show us the butterfly within himself that would spread its wings in us when we follow him in our own truth and awaken from our sleep. He said he must go away; otherwise, we would look ever to him, the man, instead of listening to our own inner Spirit as teacher.

In the composite of his teachings Jesus introduced us to the concept of the second coming. The second coming has been proclaimed for over 2,000 years, and humanity waits in faith for the return of the man Jesus. Who is to say he will not return? Certainly not I. But, we can embrace a new understanding of a second coming as offered through his teachings of the unity with our own indwelling Christ Spirit. When we do this, the second coming takes place when we awaken one morning, gaze into the mirror of our own eyes, and see his promises kept: "... [L]o, I am with you always..." (Matt. 28:20); "In that day you will know that I am in my Father, and you in me, and I in you." (John 14:20); "... I will come again and will take you to myself, that where I am you may be also." (John 14:3); "... [T]he Holy Spirit, whom the Father will send in my name, he will teach you all things, and bring to your remembrance all that I have said to you." (John 14:26) The 'I' of each individual is the indwelling Christ as it is in Jesus. It is the Light of the world that enlightens every man, woman, and child. It is the single I, and when you see with this single I, in that day will you know you are one. In that day Christ comes again, and the Holy Spirit, moving in Grace, is the agent of that coming.

The dawning of that day has proven to be an evolutionary journey and not a one-time event for most of us. As we look at the life of Jesus we see his admonition to "follow me" was our first clue that the second coming would be a journey into the soul. He was born a child, educated, and taught. He was baptized, and in that baptism the Holy Spirit descended in consciousness to activate a process of remembering his destiny, mission, and purpose that empowered him to do a mighty work and eventually overcome the last enemy—death. His journey is our journey, from birth, to baptism, to crucifixion (the metaphor for the final crossing out—the death of all illusions of separation); and then to resurrection, transfiguration, and, finally, into ascension.

This journey requires trust, devotion, pure heart intention, and a willingness to surrender all to God I Am. It is a journey through the mountains and valleys of the shadows of the death of the ego, all illusion, and sense of separation. To the degree you can recognize this as a journey of Love and completely surrender and accept it, resisting nothing on your path, it will be a journey of Peace, Love, and Joy. Christ is coming in you, spiraling, climbing, and expanding—making its way to the throne of consciousness wherein it will rule and make all things new by taking its position of Divine inheritance.

Baptism of the Conscious and Subconscious

Conscious mind must first accept its destined right position which is not to originate choice, but to accept choice impulsed from its Source—the superconscious or what I call Gracemind. This is definitely the most difficult repentance of change to accept and actualize because it is a complete reversal of traditional understanding. You are acclimated to making all your choices at the level of conscious awareness which thinks its perceptions, beliefs, and positions are gospel. The truth of the matter is, conscious perceptions may or may not be in alignment with truth, but regardless of their degree of truth, your gift of freewill choice was never designed to *originate* here. It was designed to originate from superconscious/Gracemind as a function of its true nature. It is the superconscious that impulses conscious choices through pure heart desire, intuition, and inner knowing. The conscious is designed to pick up the impulse after it has been sent and to run with it. It is the catcher of the ball, not the pitcher. Then, in order for there to be a home run, there must be no enter-fear-ence from the field. The conscious' true function is the freewill choice of follow-through.

At first, this will take a lot of practice and determination. The conscious has assumed a position in the field of consciousness it is simply not qualified to handle. It will take a total commitment of pure humility and love from you in order to convince it that it has misunderstood its mission. There are two possible choices the conscious will be facing as it hears news of this information. One, it can feel rejected, threatened, out of control, and judged—this is the egoic position. The second choice is for it to accept its much greater purpose of being the gift of freewill choice within the Will of God, not *free* will as being independent on its own. Wow, what a difference. The conscious is the synthesizing mechanism that can function as the agent of acceptance of the fulfillment for God's Will. "I choose to choose the Will of God I Am!" Say that again. Close your eyes; say it one more time! "I choose to choose the Will of God I Am!" This is the epitome of freewill choice and automatically adjusts the conscious to its right-full position of function.

As soon as the conscious completely *accepts* its originally designed functional position, there will be no resistance and, therefore, no pain and suffering due to a sense of loss. Pain and suffering come from an ego state that believes something valuable is being surrendered. Ego disintegrates automatically when the elixir of truth is poured upon its content. This corrected positioning eliminates a possibility of baptism by fire or any wilderness experience. It accepts the baptism of Gracemind through Holy Spirit regeneration. The conscious then basks in the Son Light, becoming a prismic Light catcher. This is what Charles Fillmore meant when he said, *"It* (the conscious) *must look ever to the superconscious for all direction and instruction. It can of itself do nothing with assurance, because the Spirit of wisdom rests in the superconscious."*

More simply stated, this means the conscious must be ever poised facing inward, listening and waiting patiently for instructions, truth, and guidance. Then it will be impulsed to choose a follow-through appropriate to the information received.

In its new position, the conscious should be made aware
it could first encounter a barrage of thoughts and feelings
surfacing from the depths of the ocean of the subconscious.
This content may not be very pretty, for there is a strong
possibility it will reflect corrupted truth that has been buried for
a long, long time. If this is the case, it may look like a variety
of things including despair, hopelessness, need for control,
need to get even, martyrdom, self-righteousness, selfishness,
indignation, unfulfilled expectations, judgments, resentments,
anger, unworthiness, superiority, inferiority, doubt, fear, worry,
impatience, addictions, co-dependences, disappointments, or
rejections. Remember, these represent the debris of illusions
imprisoned in the ghettos of consciousness which have been
compressed as subconscious memories. If simply observed,
instead of being attacked or attached in any way, they will
either drift away with the tides never to be seen again or drown
in the living waters of truth. If they surface, it is for a spiritual
purpose which will make room for the Son Light to completely
fill the space left in the wake of their emptying. In this way,
you eliminate the dredging and accept the healing of the
subconscious by way of Grace. This saves lifetimes of aimless
journeying in circles and dramatically accelerates the awakening
process.

Every individual's experience of the baptism will be unique.
The length and intensity is directly proportional to the density of
illusory content being tenaciously held in the subconscious. The
resistance of your conscious mind to yield its position, and the
willingness of you, the aspirant, to change and be non-resistant
to change will directly affect your transformation.

You may have been experiencing the baptism for several
lifetimes and, as a result, encounter only a small residue of
illusory content. A clue that this is true for you will be the
natural flow of Peace, Love, and Joy that is, by and large,
effortless. You are the Light bearers who are now assisting
others. Thank you for the work you have done in other lifetimes
and this one. We are very grateful you are here assisting all
of humanity. If you are one of these Beloveds, there will be

no judgment or lack of compassion expressed by you toward those who are still being baptized. Others will find this processing continues for an extensive period of time. If it is of any consolation to you, my baptism is still in effect after forty years. It consciously began in my twenties, intensified in my forties and fifties, and now feels more like a process of monthly maintenance with fragments of ancient baggage still surfacing here and there.

Try to remember that Metaphysical Mind is going to have a tendency to want to analyze, rationalize, and reason with all the content that surfaces. It is like a curious cat whose nature is to explore every little bit of debris, nook, and cranny.

To accelerate your processing and experience the least amount of resistance (baptism by fire), allow yourself to move into Mystic Mind awareness which is activated by a deep desire to surrender. *Let surrender **be not** a process of the need to let go, but the **willingness to accept** what surfaces.* With this awareness you function from Master Mind, and in Master Mind there is no concept of surrender as a process whereby something is taken from you. ***Surrender is equal to acceptance.*** Acceptance is the precursor of non-resistance. Non-resistance is neutral to *whatever* is presenting itself. If the 'whatever' is based in Reality, it will multiply its goodness from the nature of its Essence; if it is not, it will dissolve into nothingness, for it has no true Source for its sustenance. This is the practice of being in the world but not of it—the way of Grace.

Holy Spirit energy is extremely powerful and follows no pathway of reasoning or set rules. It is personal to each individual as it rotor-rooters its way through the subconscious, devouring everything in its path like a ravenous 'Pac man.' As it does this, it infuses everything with its Essence, transforming it into the image and likeness of itself. It is like the waving of the magic wand of Cinderella's fairy godmother that changed Cinderella and all her needs to reflect her destiny of "happily ever after."

At one point in my own baptismal process, I kept hearing the word *infusion*, so I looked it up. Webster revealed it to be *"the continuous slow introduction of a solution into a vein ... to pour in ... to cause to be permeated with something (as a principle or quality) that alters for the better ... to steep in liquid (as water) without boiling for extracting useful qualities ... to introduce one thing into another so as to affect it throughout."* (Webster Unabridged)

As I correlated this with my own personal experience of the Holy Spirit, I realized that baptism is an infusion process, and that it needs to be slow because the infilling infuses an extremely high frequency of energy that unlocks the kingdom or Christ consciousness within, filling understanding with a whole new perspective of Reality. It takes time for this new awareness to make a safe shift in consciousness within the mind, body, and its cellular memory. This helps you to be more patient and trusting of your individual progress.

Slow infusion of baptismal energies from the Holy Spirit can also be related to Webster's use of the word, *alters*. It causes one to be permeated with the Christ principle which *alters* for the better. When Holy Spirit begins alterations on you, it does an *extreme makeover*. It rips everything apart and puts it back together again as a new creation, to such a degree that you don't even recognize the old. It turns everything inside out, upside down, and finally right side up. It transforms old wine skins (old beliefs) and induces new wine—truth. You don't receive just a face lift; you receive an *extreme makeover*, an entire new body in Christ.

Holy Spirit infuses a high spiritual realization of truth into awareness as it comes in contact with any old error belief. This has the potential to create a conflict, not at the level of the old error belief, but at the level of *you*, the *beholder of* the belief. If you are tenacious—resistant to its demise—you will experience much distress and discomfort. Illusion, by its nature, will disappear when faced with the truth. Truth always replaces the face in the mirror with a reflection of itself. It is not the error belief that wants to hold on. It is you who hold the error belief.

You are tenacious as an effect of your belief that letting anything go may result in loss. You are the one, my Love, who must now *accept* the new wine as its replacement. Your *acceptance* of the new becomes the 'letting go' of the old. This is surrender through Grace. The new wine is congruent with its Source which is truth. The new wine offers you joy and happiness, for it is uninhibited by the resistors of any illusion.

When you incorporate this part of Webster's definition, "*to steep in liquid as water without boiling for extracting useful qualities,*" you realize that is exactly what is going on during baptism. The Holy Spirit is extracting the Christ—the useful qualities of the soul—drawing this consciousness into being, *without boiling*, without fire (pain and suffering). This is the consciousness from which Jesus taught as he admonished us not to toil and spin or wail and gnash our teeth. He even said, *"Take no thought..."* "Don't worry, be happy!"

Let's look at the use of the word *solution* in the context of metaphysical understanding: "the continuous slow introduction of a *solution* into a vein." Metaphysically, *solution* can be interpreted as the problem solver. That is what the Holy Spirit is all about—solving the problem of the human condition brought on by a state of consciousness that perceives separation from God—outside the trinity somehow. This is the adversary, friend—the so called *devil*—the tempter. This belief represents the 'fall' from Grace that keeps you seeing things upside down by positioning the functions of Mind inappropriately. The Holy Spirit is helping you see things rightly—right-us-ly. S/he is infusing Christ consciousness into your veins so that you may naturally stop all mental activity at the conscious level, which is simply not qualified to perceive things righteously. Holy Spirit infusion is the *solution* to the whole human condition.

Infusion means to *pour in*. Emerson says, "[w]e are the inlet and may become the outlet of all there is in God." Can you picture the free flow of this idea? As the Holy Spirit begins to infuse the Christ consciousness into your awareness, defusing, transforming, and removing old debris, you become the inlet and the outlet of the only begotten Son. You naturally flow as an inlet of Peace, Love, Joy, power, strength, health, and wholeness, and an outlet of the same. There is a continuous current of Divine ideas, Divine desires, Divine dreams, and Divine fulfillment. Life becomes effortless: no struggle, no wailing and gnashing of teeth—no thought. The in-pouring and outpouring of Spirit builds an effortless momentum that freely Niagaras from your inner Source.

It is important to become aware of the symptoms of Holy Spirit baptism so that you will not be afraid should you begin to have experiences outside the 'norm.' These symptoms have not only been reported by Christians but by people of all faiths and religious persuasions. They seem to be on the increase as we collectively advance within the Age of Grace. It is comforting to realize you are not going through baptism alone, even though you may feel alone at the time. If you are having any of these symptoms, gift yourself with reading material that will support you. The following list will prove helpful during this process.

Symptoms of Holy Spirit Baptism

1. **Emotional outbursts of energy:**
   You may experience a flood of tears as the superconscious/Gracemind washes away the memories of sadness associated with the past. You may have feelings of emptiness, loss, confusion, or apathy resulting from old thought patterns no longer occupying space in awareness. Actual experiences of the past that generated these patterns may or may not be revealed by the Holy Spirit. It has been my experience, as I witnessed infusion in myself and many students I have worked with, that only what is absolutely relevant to Love's expansion will be made known.

2. **Changes in the body:**
   The body may respond with a cold, diarrhea, rash,

headache, or old disease pattern emergence. Tingling
sensations, skin sensitivity, and itching have been
reported.

3.   **Changes in energy levels:**
        Surges of high energy with no need for sleep,
        combined with periods of low energy and the need for
        intervals of deep rest or sleep, is a common physical
        paradox.

4.   **Kundalini:**
        Spiritual practices may awaken the fire energy of the
        Holy Spirit. This energy is the great purifier of Spirit
        that begins a subtle inner process, which ultimately
        leads to a remembered state of union with the Divine.
        Burning sensations, as the Holy Spirit purifies the
        energy centers in the body, are common and very
        distinct from 'hot flashes,' ladies. This is baptism by
        fire but should not be feared. Fear is what contributes to
        the *experience* of baptism as being perceived as 'fiery.'
        Extremes of hot or cold within a few minutes or waves
        of heat as a prolonged continuum are common.

5.   **Involuntary body movements:**
        These movements include jerking, accordion breath,
        movement of limbs, or rocking. They may *all* come
        and go over a period of years. They may occur more
        frequently during meditation, rest, or sleep for some
        people. Jerking, swaying, shaking, rapid head rotation,
        tremors, feeling an inner force pushing you into
        postures, or moving your body in unusual ways—all
        are not to be feared. Heart flutterings, rapid eye
        movement, speaking in tongues, toning, or uttering
        Sanskrit is the experience of some seekers. A bizarre
        experience often reported: uncontrollably laughing one
        minute and crying the next without a clue as to why.

6. **Heightened spiritual sensitivity:**
   Clairvoyance, clairaudience, inner dimensional
   viewing, heightened ESP, visions of light, symbols,
   colors, auras, entities, or review of past life
   experiences may visit you. There may be a stimulation
   of the olfactory system with perceptions of scents of
   sandalwood, rose, or incense, or you may experience
   feeling bigger than the body or having an out-of-
   body experience. Immense joy and compassion, inner
   knowing, oneness, heightened intuition—all are
   reported as encounters of this holy time.

7. **Dreams:**
   You may have strange dreams, reoccurring dreams,
   nightmares, or even prophetic dreams.

8. **Sex:**
   There my be an increase in the desire for sexual
   pleasures, or there may be a lessening of sexual desire.
   Both of these will be brought into balance as soon
   as your mental, emotional, and physical bodies are
   aligned.

9. **Major life changes:**
   Change, change, change is the effect of this
   infusion, especially in relationships, careers, beliefs,
   perceptions, and desires. "Be prepared" is the Scout's
   motto!

Beloved, you are being infused with the Light of the world
that you are. It is downloading itself to make itself known and
positioning itself upon the throne of your mind to make all
things new. This is your destiny!

Have you ever asked yourself what it means to be the
Light of the world? Just look at how Webster defines *light* as it
is experienced in this world. Then let this definition become a

metaphor to help you make a quantum leap in understanding your eternal Self as the Light of the world referenced by Jesus: *"luminous energy, radiant energy; ... electromagnetic radiation ranging in wavelength from about 4 thousand to 7,700 angstrom units and propagated at a speed of about 186,300 miles per second; ... considered variously as a wave, corpuscular, or quantum phenomenon; ... an illuminating agent or source; ... a gleam or sparkle, as in the eyes; means of igniting, as a spark, flame, match, or the like; ... state of being visible, exposed ... or revealed to brighten ... with joy, animation, or the like; ... take fire or become kindled; ... brighten with animation or joy"* (Webster Unabridged)

The baptism of the Holy Spirit is the infusion of the Light of Christ consciousness which I call Gracemind or Master Mind. You are literally being revealed as the 'Light of the world,' the *Word* made flesh, the image and likeness, the only begotten son or daughter of God. This is a glorious time for you. It is the promise kept of the Second Coming. Rejoice and be glad in it!

The Virgin State ~ Reconciling Opposites

The virgin state of Mind is beyond all polarity but inclusive of it. Once the baptism is complete, this will become the resting state of your mind. It is difficult to convey an understanding of this state with words because the virgin state is the unified field of consciousness from and in which all polarity rests and emerges. It is virgin of the capacity to judge, being all inclusive, accepting infinite possibilities of extremes within the unity out of which all polarity is possible.

The following is a group of words descriptive of opposites and an attempt to identify the unity out of which each emerges. As the conscious and subconscious are cleared of all judgment, even-exchange ideas and perceptions of value, the consciousness of unity from which opposites appear becomes the awareness of the aspirant. Gracemind perceives only unity. Take a look at these opposites and then recognize the unified field from which they express. The opposites are neither good nor bad, right or wrong, they are simply possibilities of extremes of the same thing.

Opposites: Extremes of possibilities		Unified Field:
Order	Chaos	**Peace**
Judgment	Acceptance	**Love**
Sadness	Happiness	**Joy**
Poverty	Wealth	**Abundance**
Rejection	Approval	**Acceptance**
Bondage	Liberty	**Freedom**
Strength	Weakness	**Power**
Doubt	Faith	**Trust**

In Holy Spirit baptism, judgment related to the expression of opposites will subside and acceptance of their expression will increase. Conscious mind, adjusting to its new position of observer and looking ever to the superconscious, will begin to experience the unified field of awareness from which all polarities of expression are possible. This is a glorious happening which gives you increasing degrees of mental, emotional, and physical freedom. Vibrations of the unified field are infinitely blissful and healing to the soul and body. These energies are nourishment for your entire Being and will ultimately create a Light body of Unity for your final ascension in consciousness. Begin even now to practice this awareness: "I am *Peace* expressing as *Love* in the consciousness of *Joy* which draws forth *Abundance* as the effect of *Acceptance* through my *Freedom* and *Power* to *Trust.*" This awareness accepts the above mentioned unified field of myriad possibilities of opposites.

I could make the list infinitely longer, but I will leave that task to you. When you identify the unity out of which all possibilities emerge, let your entire Being rest in the unity. You will be absolutely amazed at the healing power of this practice as it ushers in the consciousness of Grace. You are identifying yourself *as* Essence instead of identifying yourself as any polarized *expression* from an infinite sea of possibilities. This effects awakening at the level of being Cause instead of attempting to awaken (heal perceptions of consciousness) from the level of effect. This shifts the journey from one of evolution, to one of revolution and revelation—a major shift in Grace Awakening Essence.

Chapter Six

Portals of Choice

Chapter 6

Portals of Choice

I Have Lived !

I have burned myself by fire 'til pain consumed my all.
I have fed myself by flame and warmed my home.
I have felt the depth of sadness disappointment offered me,
And the height of joy from a blessing given or received.

I have laughed so hard time stood still
And cried so deeply eternity was its measure.
I have felt so tired my breath was labored in its resting,
And so full of Life that impossible was as easy as breathing.

I have judged and criticized.
I have condemned and blamed.
I have ridiculed and scorned.
I have lied.

I have loved without condition and accepted without question.
I have approved and forgiven.
I have been merciful and selfless.
I have been honest.

I have doubted and wavered in uncertainty.
I have had faith beyond the reasoning mind.
I have controlled and been controlling.
I have surrendered all.

My heart has ached with passion's dream.
I have been consumed by the emptiness of the desireless state.
I have felt the depths of stupidity and the inability to understand.
I have marveled at my wisdom and its knowing beyond the
mind.

I have felt as large as the cosmos, as small as a grain of sand.
I have experienced the unity of belonging
and loneliness of rejection.
I have been accused and found guilty in my innocence.
I have been pardoned and forgiven in my guilt.

I have felt bondage. I have felt freedom.
I have felt jealousy to the point of rage.
I have felt love that passeth understanding.
The depths of fear have paralyzed my soul.
The miracle of peace has healed my fear.

I have gained and lost.
I have accepted, and I have rejected.
I have saved a life from extinction taking spider to the door.
I have killed a million flies.

I have felt God's presence nearer than breathing.
I have questioned if there was a God.
I have survived a thousand deaths.
I have lived.

~ ~ ~

The outpouring of my heart as I wrote the above helped me
to realize I have lived, and I have lived to witness the reflections
of my greatest gift, the gift of choice. I am a creator, created in
the image and likeness of my God Essence. With the birth of
me as Essence, my inheritance is freewill. I can not abandon
my freewill nature. I can not escape the mind's choosing and
the feelings my mind generates any more than I can escape my
next breath. It is in my blood. It is in my genes. It is in my mind,
heart, and soul. Choosing is as automatic as the beat of my heart,
as forever as Life itself. With this inheritance I have traveled,
explored, searched, journeyed, and experienced upon this sweet
Earth through each phase of the journey circle. With this gift
I have experienced an infinite number of possibilities within
extremes and witnessed the consequences of those choices.

Yes, dear ones, I have lived, and so have you, but now we enter into an even greater capacity of living—living with conscious understanding of our gift of freewill.

Over time, choice has become a subject of great confusion for the sincere aspirant. Understanding choice is an evolutionary process that begins with Mortal Mind. Mortal Mind sees itself as separate from God and therefore views *free will* choice as isolated and independent of Source. Metaphysical Mind still acknowledges *free will* choice at the level of independence but expands the understanding to recognize the choices of *free will* determine the individual's *experience* of life. Mystic Mind begins to merge the concept of *free will* from being a will independent of God's Will, to *freewill* as being the freedom of choice within the one and only Will of God I am. This recognition is the motivation for constant surrender and acceptance during the metamorphosis of Mystic Mind. As surrender completes itself in the mystic, the mystic realizes surrender is the choice for the awareness of **unity** that draws forth the Divine Destiny, plan, and individuated code of Essence written in the heart. Finally, the full awakening in Master Mind is the awareness of *freewill* as being the choice activity *of* the superconscious/Gracemind functioning true to its nature. In the absolute, God is *choice* itself, and we are *that* in our absoluteness. This is the ultimate awareness of choice recognized by Mind united and functioning as designed.

Throughout your spiritual awakening journey, you will experience varying degrees of understanding related to choice. So, let's embrace a study of choice by recognizing and examining these degrees with the goal in mind of integrating them into the depth of your capability to understand. This integration will greatly assist you in reconciling opposites, seeing with the *single* eye of Christ, and beholding the unity of all life. I have identified the awakening degrees of choice understandings as *portals*, for I see them as openings within Gracemind that beckon us to step through to receive greater and greater gifts of wisdom and love.

Portal No. 1: Influences of Choice

There are many factors of influence that contribute to exercising your gift of freewill choice. At first glance some of them seem to be beyond the gift of freewill. In Grace awakening you are exploring a new definition of freewill as the capacity to accept the Will (movement of Love) of God's Divine Plan written in your heart. Grace reveals that many of the factors you believed to be choice-makers *for you* are not choice-makers but *influences* you continue to give power. Some of these influences are perceived as astrological determinants for destiny, physical inherited DNA, karma, and belief systems entrenched in memory. Let's look at each of these from the eyes of Grace.

Astrological birth signs are not determinants of destiny, and therefore, not choice-makers aligned with the power of freewill. They are the vibrational frequencies most aligned with *your* consciousness which support or match your spiritual DNA *and* your karmic belief systems gathered from the, so called, awakening in time. Your collective vibrational consciousness chose the moment of your birth through the frequency of energy most aligned with the collective astrological energy pattern upon the Earth that was the closest match to your consciousness. As the stars, planets, and essence of the heavens continually wave and particle themselves into the Earth's systems of life, their combined energies are attracted by your predominant, collective, vibrational frequencies in every given moment. These are powerful energies of influence. They are no different from the strong influence of your current home environment—family, work, friends, and habitual thoughts that generate feelings and emotions. The energies of the cosmic universe always support and are attracted by the laws of abundance, acceptance, and freedom as they are being expressed through your consciousness. Astrology does not hold or dictate your destiny. If it did, it would be your God. Nor does it make choices for you, unless, through your belief, you give it the power. The astrological set up is an energetic expression of God energies supportive of all ideas manifested and manifesting within the laws of consciousness. The only determinant of your destiny is the Divine idea of you. It begins and ends there!

What about karma? Karma is the experience or the effect of the consequences of choices made in the past that continue to influence choices of the present. Every moment of your existence you are either choosing your Divine Destiny or your karma. If you are living from the laws of karma, then of course karma becomes your destiny. It's that simple. Consciousness is eternal and perpetually operative within you as creative principle. The gift of freewill empowers you to take thought and focus. To the degree that you choose your Divinity through acceptance do you align your awareness with your Divine nature and create an environment in your mind which accepts and attracts the Divine Plan, Divine Will, and Divine Destiny. Peace is at the center of this choice, Love is the expression of this choice, and Joy is the effect of this choice.

Karma is the effect of the wheel of thought that has formed a nucleus around your dreams, visions, desires, fears, and belief systems of the past, present, or perceived future. In order for the wheel of thought to become karmic, it must first become habitual and clothed with feelings that have become deeply impressioned in memory. These patterns of thoughts and feelings may or may not be conscious and can be either positive or negative in nature. Those that have been deeply suppressed are usually not recognized by you until your mind bends into memory. Clues for you that indicate you are functioning in negative karma will show up in the experience of life as struggle, worry, anger, low self esteem, poverty, illness, doubt, anxiety, and other heartbreaking states. You may also be living in fear, confusion, and judgment, intensifying a sense of separation from Divine Will. By the law of attraction, this calls into experience more of what you don't want and delays manifestation of destiny's unfolding. Round and round you go living in a karmic spin much like a loose screw spinning in grooves of warped threads. Karma ceases to be an influence of choice as soon as the habitual spinning of the habits of focus, memory, and futuring stop! "Stop spinning," is the cry from Grace. It is much like the gaining of weight from a habitual pattern of eating foods that contribute to the fat producing process of the body's chemistry. If you continue to eat the same as you always have, your karmic experience will be the continuation of gaining weight. As soon as you stop eating the same foods, combinations of foods, and amounts of foods, the weight gain stops and eventually reverses itself to reflect the new patterns being implemented. Einstein's definition of insanity is worth mentioning here: "Insanity is doing the same thing over again and expecting different results."

Nobody seems to be concerned about good karma, and that is as it should be, for good karma always reflects some measure of consciousness functioning from Grace. But there will come a time when even good karma will pale as a desired experience compared to coming face to face with the treasures of Grace. Grace is not determined by degrees of focus upon Divinity, but by Divinity recognized as *you*. Grace is not sustained by any thought, feeling, or emotion—it is effortlessly sustained by its own Essence. It is not circular—not a return—but a forever expansive awakening, a continual 'never before' experience of itself. It is not fueled by memory, but fueled from the original seed of infinite possibilities of Divine ideas.

What about physical DNA? Are you destined to live from this inheritance? Your physical DNA is the grand passing of the grail as the out-picturing of *consciousness* from one generation to another. Every strand of your physical DNA has at its center the memory of its original keeper. DNA memory is a very strong influence within your body structure as well as in your mental and emotional nature. You may have read about or witnessed someone who has received a transplanted organ from another human being in an effort to replace one that was worn out. The recipient often reports having cravings and impulses that were completely foreign to them before the transplant but were very prevalent in their donor. The entire collective consciousness of every individual is contained within every cell of their bodies. This consciousness is passed on through copulation. This does not mean one's life is destined to continue to express its influence. Remember, your Divine inheritance is Peace, Love, and Joy. These components of spiritual consciousness are far superior to the frequencies of your physical DNA. When you accept the consciousness of Grace as your only inheritance, the energy of this consciousness downloads into the mental, emotional, and physical systems to miraclize any lower vibrations in its path. Physical DNA is the fulfillment of the scriptural promise that the sins of the fathers are visited upon the children. Spiritual DNA is the fulfillment of the scriptural promise that "... *grace and truth came through Jesus Christ.* ... *And from his fullness,* **have** *we* **all received***, grace upon grace."* (John 1:16) The Grace of the Father is visited upon the children of our present, past, and future. Because of our oneness we all experience healing. *"... and I, when 'I' am lifted up from the earth, will draw* **all** *men to myself."* (John 12:32) I have often said the healing of the children is visited upon the fathers. Praise God!

Portal No. 2: Choice from the Fountain of Trust

Your experience of Peace, Love, and Joy—your abundance, your expression of creativity, your degree of happiness and fulfillment—are all directly proportional to your capacity to trust! From your center of trust, Grace unfolds and makes known your destiny and the Divine Plan for your life. Trust is the way of revelation by Grace and the ultimate choice of choices from the corrected positioning of the conscious mind looking ever to the superconscious.

Trust is the lesson of all lessons and the goal of all goals in living a fulfilled life. All of earth's lessons can be embraced and fully realized by one who is focused in trust. Your capacity to love is directly proportional to your capacity to trust. Your capacity to express the Divine gifts and attributes of your individuated God Self is directly proportional to your capacity to trust. The healing of body and soul is miraclized by your capacity to trust. Trust is the ultimate of all choices—the

supreme boundlessness of mind, heart, and soul. It is the
highest vibrational choice of all choices. Its effect is Grace,
and from the center of Grace all life exists, unfolds, and fulfills
itself according to original design. Your freedom is directly
proportional to your capacity to trust, and your evolution
depends on it. Your Essence commands it.

Trust is the natural flow of Essence. For most, however,
this trusting awareness is not a steady stream of consciousness.
Instead, trusting is a roller coaster ride in the amusement park
of life. Up and down, high in faith one moment and lost in the
pit of the stomach the next. Why, I ask myself, is this true? Why
is it so difficult to have a steady stream of faith and trust like
a river flowing peacefully from its Source? Why is trust not
as automatic to mind as breath is to body? Why, if trust is the
essential resting place of Mind in alignment with the true nature
of Being, is it not the manger of the soul? Why does one not live
in a natural state of trust all the time, and how can one awaken to
this natural state?

One of the reasons you vacillate in your capacity to trust
is because you are *confused* about what you *believe*. Your
belief system is continually being challenged by the moment's
experience. When experiences don't reconcile with your beliefs,
at best you are tempted to waver and doubt; at worst, you are
devastated and fall into deep depression or a state of helpless
hopelessness. Challenges to your belief system trigger your
deepest fears. This in turn motivates responses and actions out
of alignment with the true nature of Essence. When your mind
is out of alignment with Essence, it is impossible to have faith
and trust. When confusion about what you believe challenges the
mind, you find yourself in pastures that are empty.

The question that follows this awareness is, 'Why are you
confused about what you believe?' One of the answers is that
the true nature of Reality is filled with seeming paradoxes.
A paradox is a statement or fact that is true, which contains
a complimentary, apparently contradictory statement or fact
which is also true. An example of a paradoxical statement would
be something like, "less is more." Being unable to reconcile a

paradox will always extend to mind an invitation to question and, thus, waver in trust. For example: let's take the paradox of destiny vs. freewill choice. Do you have total freewill, or are certain aspects of life pre-determined? If you can't reconcile these seemingly opposite concepts, it will be impossible for you to trust your freewill choices, your goals, dreams, and visions without questioning if they are in alignment with what is destined for you within God's Will. The confusion around this paradox alone is responsible for much of your inability to trust.

Take a moment to think about all the trust issues this paradox brings up for you about relationships, work, job opportunities, mission and purpose, truth, questions about life and death, etc. Are you destined to marry a certain person, or do you have freewill choice, and does it really matter in the grand scheme of things? Should you take a job that has been offered you, or should you hold out for something else that is perhaps more in alignment with your destined expression of your individual gifts and talents? Is the time of your death predetermined or do the choices you make in life create the windows of opportunity for your exit? I know of a man who recently committed suicide. Was that freewill choice, or was it his destiny? You can see the depth of confusion that is possible when you examine these paradoxes, and how confusion about your understanding can throw you into a lack of faith and trust.

Trust is not a verb which gives reference to doing. It is a sacred noun synonymous with the true nature *of* Being. Absolute trust is not subject to qualifiers. Trust, at the level of Essence, is not about putting trust *in* something, even something as sacred as life, Divine Plan, or your concept of God. Meaning given to these words will differ according to the individual mind holding such ideas. For example, what would you say if I asked you to define God, life, or Divine Plan? My definitions and your definitions, I promise you, will not be the same, and, therefore, for me to try to trust God from your perspective would be as impossible as it would be for you to trust God from my perspective. In addition, trusting God from my *perspective* has proved to me to be impossible because my *perspective* may embrace many questions of doubt and confusion. How about your perspective of God? My point is, no wonder you vacillate in the ability to trust, for you vacillate in the understanding of what you put your trust in. This is a portal of wisdom that every Beloved must walk through. It is indicative of Gracemind awakening.

You are, however, quite capable of *being* trust, for trust is an expression of the *nature* of your *Essence*. You are being asked to *put your trust in trust itself,* which *is* the nature of who you are. A good example of this kind of trust can be observed in the Nature Kingdom. Nature trusts because it does not question or believe. It remains in a state of total peace, non-resistance, and complete acceptance. This is what it means for you to trust— nothing more and nothing less. One of my favorite definitions of trust via the word 'faith' is a quote from Dr. Rabindranath Tagore, the late Nobel poet laureate and philosopher of India: "*Faith is the bird that feels the light and sings when the dawn is still dark.*" This is the experience of one who is flowing from the Divine nature of trust.

Now let me reiterate my opening paragraph: "Your experience of Peace, Love, and Joy—your abundance, your expression of creativity, your degree of happiness and fulfillment—are all directly proportional to your capacity to trust, and, from your center *of* trust, Grace unfolds and makes known your destiny and the Divine Plan for your life." Thus, you are on an awakening journey of Grace into the Essence of Being whose nature is one of pure, absolute trust as *you* step through the portal of your Self into *What Is.* So now step with me through the portal of the agony and the ecstasy of belief.

Portal No. 3: Choice from the Agony and Ecstasy of Belief

Ultimately, you will come to a place in awareness where you begin to glimpse the great truth that trust, as your true nature, can never be sustained by a belief system of any kind. Your belief system is always vacillating and changing. You cannot, with absolute confidence of knowing, put your faith and trust in any perception that vacillates. *The very nature of the word 'trust' implies the absence of reason, the absence of belief, and the presence of Essence.*

Belief is the movement of consciousness that functions as the catalyst for experience and expression. According to your belief, relatively speaking, will be your *experience* of Reality, which in turn will spawn another or similar belief. Your beliefs become your *experience* of Reality, not Reality itself. Mind is endlessly expansive as to the amount of belief it can hold, and, thus, endless in the possibilities of experience. Throughout the course of many lifetimes you have embraced various beliefs, exchanged one for another—questioning, analyzing, contextualizing, and synthesizing belief, belief, belief. These structures have been tried on and taken off as the garments of your soul. They have expressed in life the fashion of your character and the experience of your drama.

Once again, you find yourself here in sweet Earth portraying the character of your accumulated beliefs, but is anything that is exchangeable or replaceable part of the nature of Reality? No, 'exchangeable and replaceable' is merely the nature of the creative process within Reality, and that is as it was designed.

Let's fully examine the role of belief in the creative process as a way of reconciling any paradoxes that may be inhibitors to trust. Belief is an energetic attractor. In and of itself it is not the creative principle within Reality. Only God is creative principle. Belief does, however, serve as a temporal mechanism of attraction because of the acceptance factor of whatever belief is held. From this perspective it is creative. God as creative principle is not subject to belief, nor is that which God creates subject to belief in it. Health is not dependant upon your belief in its existence. Health is the natural outpouring of Life. Life is not dependent upon your belief. Life is eternal. Power is not dependent upon your belief. Power is always available to all. Love is not dependent upon your belief in it. Love is the forever of the heartbeat of God. I'm sure you get the idea. Your *experience,* however, of any and all of that which is eternal, will be determined by the concept of the qualifiers you entertain through your belief system.

God as creative principle is the movement of the matrix of Essence, and by its own nature creates according to the design of the principle. It is designed to manifest. To the brain mind that perceives this world as dualistic, belief is relevant as the agent of choice and out-pictures a world of seeming opposites. To the Mind that *exists* (not perceives) in a unified world, belief is not relevant. Uninhibited by belief, God, as creative principle will automatically manifest the perfection of Essence and mirror to you an experience of life equal to that design.

If all is truly one, already one, perfect in expression, what is there to believe in? Your immediate response may be to believe in the oneness, but the concept of oneness, from a dualistic mind, always contains the possibility of a world of separation. Oneness is not dependent upon your awareness, for it is not perceivable. Perceivability is an activity of the mind which requires a subject and an object for comparison. Oneness cannot be perceived by comparison. It is only perceivable from itself—from what it is, not from what it is not. Therefore, any belief you may be carrying as content of mind within the *concept* of oneness is not Reality, it is a perception *of* Reality. When life is viewed from perception, perception is the experience and may or may not be reflective of eternal truth. Such is the agony and the ecstasy of belief.

Now, here is the paradoxical good news: when a belief is focused in the direction *of* the Eternal, the magnetic attraction of the Eternal is expedient in manifestation, for it encounters no resistance in the form of illusion. If what you believe is true to Reality, the Reality of that which is believed will remain and sustain itself. The practice of believing aligned with truth is a powerful tool to activate *acceptance* at the level of your conscious and subconscious mind. This is what Charles Fillmore meant when he expressed the importance of the conscious mind cooperating with the superconscious.

If what you believe is not reflecting an expression of Reality, the illusion will be sustained only by your belief. Here is how you can determine if what you believe is true to the nature of Reality: when you withdraw your belief in whatever, does the *whatever* remain or fall away? Examples of expressions of Reality are life, health, beauty, abundance, laws of creation, and Peace, Love, and Joy. Examples of expressions of non-reality or illusions are lack, sickness, disharmony, separation, duality, right and wrong, and good and bad. Surrender all belief in these concepts and see if they don't just disappear. Without belief there is nothing to sustain them.

This explains how the truisms around the concepts of belief remain unaltered, but from a totally different perspective. You have heard it said, "Your belief has made you well;" "According to your belief will it be done unto you;" and "Thoughts held in your mind, produce after their kind." No, Beloved, I am not discrediting these idioms of truth. Belief does serve as a temporal mechanism of attraction to the perceived reality in a world of seeming paradoxes, opposites, and dualism.

If you will carefully examine your beliefs as you have applied them to your *perceptions* of truth, you will see how they have functioned for you as magnetic attractors of either truth or illusion. They have been magnetic attractors proportionate to your degree of acceptance of them relative to your *perception* of any idea, dream, desire, or concept. In this way your beliefs have kept you in an experience of life directly proportional to the measure of your perception.

Living from belief is living in karma, and sometimes *in* Grace, but it is not living *from* Grace. Living *from* Grace is an eternal principle of Love expressing as consciousness true to the Essence of its nature. As such, Grace needs no belief, nor is it *subject to* your belief. This is similar to the ideas of living *from* Love, Peace, and Joy, vs. living *in* love, peace, and joy. Living *from* is living *as*, or Source. Living *in* implies relationship and is subject to perceptions. Big difference—not that living *in* is not good, but living *from* is Grace Awakened as God Essence. Living *in* is subject to *out*. You can fall *in* love and *out* of love according to perceptions and conditions placed upon the fall, but living *from* Love is an entirely different experience. It is conditionless and requires no belief—it is *from* Essence. To the degree your belief is aligned with the truth of the nature of Reality does truth remain in your life without effort.

So where does that put belief in the creative process and in your life? Belief is an activity of Mortal, Metaphysical, and Mystic Mind. It facilitates understanding, reasoning, and a desire for surrender. It is important because it serves as a magnetic attractor of that to which it points. If your belief is focused **on** truth, absent any illusory perception, then truth will attract itself to you in its totality.

Belief absent of content is trust. This may seem somewhat paradoxical but in Reality it is easily reconcilable. For now, let your belief serve in your awareness as a conditioner of consciousness which is making ready for the seeds of Reality to emerge in full bloom. Let your beliefs be recognized as the non-resisters of truth which accept the Ineffable. Remove from your belief the idea that the power is in the belief, and place your trust in that to which the belief points. Your Divinity will reveal its kingdom from the nature of what it is. It needs no help from you other than non-resistance.

Portal No. 4: Choice from the Frequency of Vibration

"Nothing rests; everything moves; everything vibrates." (*The Kybalion*) This is ancient Hermetic doctrine that was recognized by early Greek philosophers who applied its truth to many of their systems. Outside of Hermetic philosophers, this great truth got buried beneath the teachings of the evolutionary processes of humanity but was rekindled in the nineteenth-century physical sciences. Today, science embraces these principles.

Everything vibrates! This is an important revelation, for it will help you grasp a deeper level of understanding choice—

choice at the level of vibration. If choices and the level of awareness from which they are made could be measured, you would see that every choice is made from the *collective* vibration *of the one choosing.*

Faster vibrations are always higher in frequency. The higher the frequency, the closer you are to the awareness of the vibrations of Essence or Spirit. In the presence of high vibrational frequencies, lower vibrational frequencies are nullified and transmuted. In-depth studies of vibrational frequencies have revealed that lower frequencies are slower in motion, more solid, and much more materialistic. As vibrational frequencies increase by identification with the true nature of Being, your vibrational frequencies rise, becoming less solid. This progression can be correlated to match the world that shows up in degrees of solidity: slower frequencies manifest as solid objects; faster frequencies become less solid or fluid; even higher frequencies express as light; and, beyond light they are not visible or measurable. These latter frequencies vibrate at the level of spiritual Source, the invisible, subjective home of Essence from which the visible is made known. Slower vibrations have a tendency to attach awareness to the world of solid form and manifestation—the experience, the situation, or the problem. As you detach from personal perceptions, opinions, judgments, and values assigned through the comparison of opposites, you raise your frequencies to the choice level of Spirit. This is a major advancement in spiritual awakening.

If your entire awareness is vibrating at the level of Gracemind, this state of Mind will choose from trust and in alignment with Divinity—the *collective* consciousness vibration that rests in absolute faith, assurance, and spiritual DNA. It would be a level of choice absent judgment, fear, or doubt—a virgin choice aligned with the true nature of Being. A choice reflective of the awareness that it is a choice impulsed from Essence for the purpose of manifesting original design and Divine Plan will quicken the vibratory correlate of *that* and bring it into expression and experience. This is an important realization because it exemplifies the fulfillment of the law of cause as effect within the principle of Grace at a very subtle level—the level of the *collective* mind.

Let's assume for a moment you are not functioning from Master Mind awareness but from Metaphysical Mind which still expresses and chooses from a collective awareness of duality. You long and yearn for a relationship—Mr. or Ms. Perfect. Your idea of that may be tall, dark, handsome, rich, agreeable, and spiritual—or petite, gorgeous, fascinating, like-minded, and wonderful. These descriptives express your perception of the *perfect* mate. However, at the level of Metaphysical Mind awareness, they are automatically inclusive of your *perception* of what you don't want—the *imperfect* mate for you. Your negative perceptions may include short, ugly, poor, argumentative, or non-spiritual, or they may gravitate toward, plain, boring, opinionated, and awful. You will attract into your life a person reflecting the average of the combined vibrations of your dualistic perceptions of perfection plus your own collective vibration of your capacity to *be* what you desire in another. More than likely your relationships will reflect the good, the bad, and the ugly—for that is the combined vibration of your collective consciousness level of choice. The law of attraction (acceptance) will find a match and invite it to come and live with you.

Now, let's assume you are functioning from Gracemind (Master Mind) awareness. Your collective consciousness would only be capable of desiring the perfect relationship for the highest good of you both. This desire would be absent any qualifiers. It would be anchored in the knowing that if you desire it, that desire is 'God-Goodness' tapping at the door of your heart to be invited in. It would rest in the assurance that the pure virgin vibration of your desire would find an equal match. Mr. or Mrs. Perfect has no choice but to accept your invitation—s/he is drawn by your pure heart vibration of unconditional Love absent good and bad qualifiers. The Law of Grace will not be mocked.

If your desire is to change any current situation or relationship, you must first elevate your collective consciousness vibration to a higher frequency. This is accomplished by withdrawing your perceptions of value and judgment upon the present situation or person and positioning the conscious mind into its natural state of stilled awareness, waiting and watching from faith, trust, and acceptance of the highest good. This position is often referenced as the observer or the witness. Practice being the observer as much as possible in any given day. The observer position of Mind is a portal all its own that will automatically lift you into the higher vibrations of your Spirit, for it raises the collective of your entire consciousness.

Ironically, the stiller the mind, the faster the frequency. The quieter the conscious mind, the more it is attracted *to and by* the higher vibrations of superconscious or Gracemind that eternally rest as stillness. Attracted by stilled awareness (non-resistance), the superconscious free-flows energies through the subconscious downloading spiritual impressions into the conscious. These vibrations of Love nullify any content or belief system that does not register at the level of Gracemind. They purify the soul. This is why deep meditation is such a powerful practice that affects transformation. Your natural position of conscious mind is stilled awareness. It is the servant, waiting for instructions— the Adam and the Eve listening for wisdom from above. Stilled awareness automatically activates the pivotal nature of conscious mind, drawing it inward, becoming stiller and stiller by way of surrendered focus for the purpose of receiving the higher frequencies of truth. From the level of Spirit, these new frequencies make themselves known to conscious mind through intuition, revelation, and impulse to spiritual action.

This is the function of the Holy Spirit—that aspect of consciousness operating as the moving force of Love that reveals, teaches, and interprets in order to effect heaven (a state of consciousness) in earth. You were born to listen, watch, and wait upon the higher frequency of Grace to come and take you to itself. This is the true meaning of being born again and the virgin birth. It is a whole new way of being in the world. As you implement choice from this practice of awareness, Gracemind sits upon the throne of your consciousness, making all things new. This not only affects change for you individually, but affects the collective raising of the consciousness of humanity as a whole.

Portal No. 5: Choice from the Nature of Unity

We live in a world of infinite possibilities of opposites in expression: *up~down, high~low, in~out, near~far, back~front, long~short, left~right, soft~hard, light~dark, fast~slow*, and I could go on *ad infinitum*. It is easy for you to look at the examples I have just given and realize they are neither good nor bad but rather samplings of infinite possibilities of expression in the created world.

You may be familiar with the saying, *"There is only one presence and one power in the universe and in my life, God the good."* It is imperative you understand the term 'good' when referencing God. God is *absolute good—the principle that never changes and is forever true to itself* in its nature and in the creative process of that nature. As *absolute good*, God is all inclusive of seeming opposites as possibilities of manifestation. Created in the image and likeness of God, infinite possibilities of creative expression are possible. These infinite possibilities are all *good* from the position of the principle at work in their capacity to manifest.

Let us shift now from looking at the myriad opposites of *measures*, to opposites considered to be *conditions: normal~abnormal, positive~negative, success~failure, rich~poor, well~sick, win~lose, smart~stupid, happy~sad, and so on.* Were you tempted to lean into judgment, exercising a mind-frame of either good or bad, or did you see these as impartially as you did opposites of *measure*? When it comes to *conditions*, the human brain is so *conditioned* to judge, it creates a fall, out of the *absolute good* state of Grace that, by its nature, accepts all. These are simply possibilities of opposites in an absolute good world. They are neither good nor bad, as a polarized mind, conditioned to believe otherwise, would infer. Now, look at what happens when you bring seemingly opposite possibilities of *virtues* to mind: *truthful~dishonest, humble~proud, giving~receiving, just~unfair.* Wow, did you witness the intensity of judgment to one being good/right and the other being bad/wrong?

Many of my students question the concept of 'neither good nor bad.' They say, "Surely there are negative polarities that are not good?" But I ask you, is there ever a time when it is good to be dishonest—when the truth would deeply hurt someone unnecessarily? How about when being proud is a sense of accomplishment vs. a hoity-toity, better-than-thou attitude? You don't have any trouble with the concept of giving and receiving, but can you say the same about justice and unfairness? How can being treated unfairly be perceived as a good thing? I have witnessed situations where someone was dealt what appeared to be an unfair hand that later proved to be the most powerful healing experience of their life. The point is not whether these things are good or bad, but that "thinking makes it so, Horatio!" These infinite possibilities of virtuous expression are all good in their potentiality of seemingly opposite movements. They do not invite judgment, rather they demand *acceptance* from the true nature of Gracemind which accepts all possibilities of expression.

There is a tendency to assign values to conditions and measures when placed in the context of positionality. These values invite judgment—the more intense the value, the more intense the judgment; the more intense the judgment, the more intense the vibration. The more intense the vibration as a negative, the more pain and suffering will be the experience. These value judgments become belief systems, which in turn determine perceptions of Reality. This is creation through the law of cause and effect. Good/bad, right/wrong are *value judgments*, and in the world of Spirit, no thing is of more or less value than another. Creation through Grace requires the absence of value judgment. It requires awareness resting at zero point where the All is One, yet infinite in its possibilities of polarities of expression.

This does not mean to become blind to a world that is

expressing these polarities inappropriately, such as abuse or harm to yourself or another. When functioning from Gracemind, you will be able to discern appropriate response to an inappropriate polarity of expression because you will be centered in unconditional Love and absolute Peace. I have never seen any wisdom teachings that say that peace and love are derived from judgment or values placed upon situations, persons, or things. The consciousness of Peace, Love, and Joy is incapable of judging or placing value. From this consciousness you will be poised in silence, absent reactive emotion, and you will respond from compassion as Spirit guides.

You are being asked to recognize the absolute goodness of God as creative principle manifesting infinite possibilities, and to accept that to every possible expression there is a time and a season of appropriateness. You may or may not be guided to *do* anything to change what is manifested or happening in the moment. Only in the absence of judgment or perceived value of any situation will you be open and receptive to the impulse of Grace to respond from Love—your Divine nature. This portal is not an easy one to step through, but until you can totally grasp its truth and be willing to function *from* this truth, you will not pass into the kingdom of Gracemind awareness of absolute trust.

Portal No. 6: Choice from the Nature of Essence

Everything created, when observed or witnessed without content of positionality from your mind, will begin to reveal *itself* from the Essence *of* itself. This revelation triggers a very high frequency in your awareness, and is often described as seeing and feeling beauty everywhere and in everything. It is an experience that is not subject to reason, for by reason what is observed may not, to the naked eye, look very beautiful.

Examples of this may be a burned down forest or a flooded housing development; a broken, twisted, or fallen tree; a lifeless carcass or corpse; a ransacked dwelling; putrefied food; garbage, litter, filth, or clutter—anything not normally seen in a positive light. Any time the eye sees what the mind *perceives* as ugly or not OK, it is simply a *mental perception* of what is observed. It is crucial you understand that these perceptions become choice makers of consciousness at the level of their vibrations, which are very slow and dense.

The spiritual 'I' sees only itself from the position of itself as the pure Essence from which the All is created. As the spiritual 'I' awakens to conscious mind by degrees, you will begin to see more and more clearly from higher frequencies of vibrations functioning as you. By their nature, these frequencies will reveal all things beautiful. You will eventually not be able to see anything less than beauty in manifestation, for you will be looking at an aspect of your Self from your Self which *is* Beauty.

Choice from the nature of Essence does not include perceptions, judgments, expectations, concepts, beliefs, sense of purpose, meaning, or values. When this awareness consumes you, your choices will naturally flow from Essence. Nothing experienced or chosen will be from a perception, or from a process of reasoning. Choice will flow naturally from your spiritual DNA—Divine Nature Attributes of Peace, Love, and Joy. This was the vibrational frequency of the choice maker in Jesus. It took no effort for him to love his enemies and bless those who persecuted him, for he was the ascended Master Mind in earth, fulfilled in his Divine remembrance of *being* what he was created to be—the Peace, Love, and Joy of God Essence expressed as image and likeness. To love was his only choice, for that is all he knew himself to be.

One of the spiritual practices we find to be incredibly transformative for those attending my retreats and workshops is to observe an object initially perceived by the beholder as ugly. The instruction is to become very still in focus—empty in mind—and simply watch and witness the object with no thought about it. You would be amazed at the tears of joy one experiences when Essence reveals itself through an object of itself to itself—especially when the object is previously perceived as something other than beautiful. This serves as a glimpse of heaven to one willing to implement this spiritual practice. It also serves as a powerful tool for healing vibrational stored *memory* of experiences of the past that are perceived as less than beautiful. Stilled witnessing is the portal for seeing with the single 'I.' Witnessing opens consciousness to the infusion of higher frequencies that become the healing agents, revolutionary catalysts, and choice-makers for awakening in Grace.

Essence also chooses from a state of Mind experienced as bliss. Bliss is a natural frequency of Essence—a natural state of Joy and happiness that flows from the true nature of Being, simply because it can't help itself. Essence houses no obstacles of resistance to its nature. When mind is empty of illusory content, *bliss infuses itself, becoming the new content* of mind that chooses from its own frequency. This is not a contrived state; it is not the effect of a reasoned perception of truth activating bliss into expression. Actually, to reason bliss into expression is impossible, for bliss is the energy of Gracemind being true to its eternal living nature. It needs no assistance, only non-resistance! Non-resistance is the effect of becoming the impartial witness.

The beauty, the magic, and the wonder of the Grace awakening process is its impeccable design. When one is living *from* Grace, any focus of *neutral observation* will draw into expression the abundance, acceptance, and freedom of a high vibrational realization of truth. In turn, any high vibrational realization of truth becomes the magnetic attractor of even greater truth. This practice is exponential in its effects of Grace awakening—forever expanding wisdom and love in understanding. For this reason, never believe for an instant you have arrived at the pinnacle of truth, for truth of its own nature is always revealing more inclusivity of itself. In this way, the journey remains an eternal awakening filled with the beauty, magic, and wonder of Grace.

Portal No. 7: Destiny's Choice

At the core of destiny's choice is the Essence of God seeking unique expression as God moves in creation. Each of you has special gifts and talents. They are the driving force at the center of the compulsion to express. The heartbeat of all your desires emanates from this Divine selection or seed code, and if you could see the tapestry of the composite Divine Plan, you would be able to grasp the importance of your contribution.

When you are not creating from this unique center, your life is miserable. When you are not following your heart's desires, creating and living from this center, you experience depression, boredom, a sense of failure, hopelessness, and dissatisfaction with life. Out of this great truth has unfolded teachings such as "do what you love, and the money will follow;" "follow your bliss;" and "take your passion, and make it happen." Beloved, this is not advice geared to get you hyped. This is the impulse of God's Will from the Divine Plan that is written in your heart. It is the 'how to' truly glorify God. Do what you love and health will follow. Do what you love and happiness will follow— harmonious relationships will follow. Do what you love and peace will follow. Do what you love and love will follow.

Exercising your unique gift of creativity, whatever that may be, is your destiny and activates the highest frequencies of consciousness in the creative process. The more creative you become, the faster the frequency of your energy field, which aligns you to the invisible world of Essence. In the presence of creativity, this vibration annuls the lower energies that produce your illusions and draws forth your destined state of Grace.

Every time I have chosen some expression outside the parameters of my spiritual gifts, I have engaged the creative process from a sense of purpose that brought me very little happiness, and I suffered. For many years I chose fields of work for the purpose of *making money* instead of following my dreams. Often, I would *settle* for something less than what brought me joy, happiness, and a sense of fulfillment.

Unhappiness, struggle, or pain and suffering are signals, wake-up calls from Essence. When these are your experience you feel orphaned from Grace. I justified suffering by believing there was a lesson in those experiences God would have me learn. I concluded it was patience, faith, trust, or to mirror concepts of Mortal Mind that needed correction. I even bought into the belief it was my karma to experience these unhappy states as a return of something I had done in the past. Well, yes, all of the above is true. Doing what I didn't love doing presented opportunities for me to understand the creative process, but they were not the *lessons God* intended for me to learn. God does not offer lessons—God offers Grace—*no mutiny from the bounty.* Suffering was simply the inevitable effect of mind choices not in alignment with the true nature of my Essence and the seed code of individual expression within that nature. It was the result of choices I had repeatedly made from the sense of separation and a confusion of beliefs. This is what constitutes karma. As soon as I chose again, and chose from my Divine seed code, karma ceased and destiny's Grace unfolded.

A word of caution: it is very important not to get caught up in the idea that written in the seed code or your book of life is the predetermined *specific expression of your gifts.* Destiny lies not in doctor, lawyer, or Indian chief, but in whatever fields of environment are conducive to the growth and maturing of your individual seed and Divine Nature Attributes. Those fields will be chosen by the collective vibration of your consciousness inclusive of your gifts and talents as awareness awakens throughout the journey. I used to believe it was my destiny to become a minister. I can see now that was not the case. My destiny was and is to do what I love to do—teach, study, and implement the concepts of Grace as they have been revealed. Ministry is a perfect outlet for my spiritual gifts. My destiny is to express the uniqueness of the seed within my individuated freedom. My destiny is to remember my unity with God as all life. My destiny is to experience the consequences of my choices in all the heavens of my creations—to become aware of myself as a creator. I could have accomplished all that in several fields, but ministry was a perfect vibrational match.

Your destiny and mine are the same, only uniquely assigned. Ultimately, you are here to accept the movement of choice *from* the Will of God's Grace as Gracemind awakens you to the full expression of your individualized Divinity.

Portal No. 8: The Ego's Last Stand: Choice from Control of No Control

The need for control keeps the ego alive and will prove to be its demise. As we have discussed throughout, going deeply into self through intention to awaken in Grace will most assuredly reveal issues of control which are powerful choice makers of limitation. This need to control contributes to the binding thread holding the emerging butterfly to any residue of what I refer to as 'caterpillarism.'

Your willingness to be out of the need to be in control of every aspect of life's offerings will sever the umbilical chord to the illusion of separation, giving final freedom to the emerging *One.* By 'out of control' I mean *living from complete and absolute trust.* The last stand of the ego proves to be a paradox that collapses egoic power. The paradox is—*it takes a lot of control to be out of control!* What do I mean by this?

Much like Sebastian in the film, *The Never Ending Story,* your earnest quest to be saved from the "Nothing" serves as the journey for understanding how to take control of your thoughts, feelings, actions, intentions, etc. Your courage to venture alone into the unknown worlds of consciousness; your faith through the Swamp of Sadness; your transparent heart that precipitated purification of your conscious and subconscious and empowered you to pass through the Oracle's x-ray vision; and finally, your willingness to step through the portal of the mirrors of your self—all took a lot of control on your part. This has also contributed to your readiness for the final demise of any separated sense of self that may try to control life, fix life, or control or fix anyone in it.

As you ascend in the awakening, the greater desire to be totally out of control at the level of your Mortal Mind and totally in control from the level of Gracemind/Master Mind will become your spiritual craving. This requires ultimate surrender of Mortal Mind awareness with relation to any and all control issues. Control *issues* and being in control of earthly responsibilities are two polarities that need to be reconciled.

Your developed capacity to be in control of many aspects of your human nature is what will empower the fulfillment of your deeper desire to be out of control to anything but your spiritual nature. To reiterate, it takes a lot of control to be out of control. When Essence is in control, the Mortal Mind is void of doubt and full of assurance. Issues, charges, and illusions cannot survive if there is no need to be in control from a sense of separation. When Essence as Gracemind is in control, it guides, directs, and aligns your choices, even little ones, with Divine Will. You are set free from confusion, indecision, and all unnecessary worry. Struggle and trying to make things happen fall away. Relationships harmonize because there is no longer a need to control them. Abundance flows into your life, for you no longer feel the need to be in control of the flow, you are the flow.

Once you desire to have Essence upon the throne of consciousness as supreme ruler, you will have the strength to stand before any sense of separation which still lingers as sustenance for the ego. You will see it for what it is, nothing! You will look deeply into the mirror of Essence and you will ask the ego (sense of separation) to gaze into the mirror with you. Your heart's desire to be out of control to anything except your Essence as your only Self will prove too strong for the ego's survival. The ego, unable to find any energy of support will not be able to see its face in the mirror and will disappear into the nothing from which it emerged. The butterfly you are will then be released from the final cord that kept it attached to the chrysalis, flying free—a new creature in Christ.

This magical movement of Grace can take place in the twinkling of an eye/I. The exact time of that twinkling can not be determined by any human efforts. Efforts to impede the moment spawn from the need to control. I do know that readiness for that final moment of surrender is precipitated by commitment, devotion, application of and dedication to the principles of Grace. The yearning of your heart to be remembered in awareness with the Eternal Divine Mind of God you are, is spawned from the Eternal Divine Mind THAT you are. Your destiny is assured.

Chapter Seven

Prayers of Grace

Chapter 7

Prayers of Grace

My soul has grown, matured, and expanded through my choices, and so has yours. But there comes a time when something *other* stirs within, a restlessness of Spirit, a despair and tiredness of experiencing the extremes of life's polarities through choice. You will yearn, as I did, to spin a cocoon around your soul and rest. You will hunger and thirst to know something more than the pendulum swing of the polarities of life. This was my yearning. It eventually becomes the yearning of every soul. I can promise you there is something more, but it requires a commitment to a life altering choice. And what is that choice? I think Trina Paulus answers that question when she was asked "How does one become a butterfly?"

"How does one become a butterfly?" she asked pensively. "You must want to fly so much that you are willing to give up being a caterpillar." ~Trina Paulus

Over the years, I have implemented many spiritual practices in pursuit of the butterfly. Each practice has blessed me, but the one that advanced my spiritual awareness more than any other is the practice of prayer from the intention of surrender which always leads to a greater degree of revelation and acceptance of truth.

I offer you now a few prayers that reflect that intention. They are indicative of the mindset of the Mystic and the Master. These prayers become invitations to the Holy Spirit for the infusion of Gracemind awareness and the defusing of all content that might be veiling that unified Mind. As these prayers become etched into your awareness, they will prove to be tremendous assets as far as conditioners of consciousness that support the purifying baptismal experience and the extinction of the judgmental perceptions of opposites. If your heart's intention can fully merge with the purity reflected in the words of these prayers, you will walk fearlessly through the valley of any shadow the ego may attempt to attach to you. You will walk with the Holy Spirit. It will not be a fire walk; instead, it will be a walk of joy and exhilaration accompanied by the deepest possible expression of faith and trust. It will be a walk equivalent to that of Peace Pilgrim in her journey around the world—a walk of Grace. Recently, the Voice of Essence expressed it to my conscious mind this way: "Walk through the gardens of earth as My Grace, and let your feet gather no moss."

The first prayer evolved through me after studying and meditating upon the experience of Jesus in crucifixion. I call it the Grace Prayer. It became clear that Jesus' experience offered much more than meets the eye. Even in his final hours he was teaching, helping us understand the power of surrender and forgiveness in the midst of all appearances. Crucifixion is the ultimate metaphor for the experience when there is doubt, fear, judgment, or any sense of separation tenaciously held while yearning for Grace awakening in Christ consciousness. As I looked long and deep into the words Jesus is reported to have spoken in the Garden of Gethsemane and on the cross, I began to see a teaching that would change my life forever.

One day I was working with surrendering my sense of personal will to the Will of God. At the beginning of my prayer I was affirming, "We are one, we are one, we are one." In the midst of praying these words over and over, a beautiful, luminous, radiant, number '1' appeared before my inner vision, and the words "we are one" echoed as if pulsating the '1,' drowning out my affirmation. The '1' appeared to be made of pure crystal, emanating an effervescent radiance beyond any light I had ever seen in this world. Then I consciously changed the prayer to the words that are attributed to Jesus in the Garden of Gethsemane as he was surrendering himself to the Will of God. He is reported to have said: *"... not my will, but thine be done."* (Luke 22:42) Similar words are recorded in *Matthew* and in *Mark*. These words never appear in *John, the Book of Love.* To my horror, as soon as I began saying "not my will, but thine be done," the 'I' turned black and began to split in two, forming a cross. Then I received this message: "When you say not *my* will, but thine be done, you imply *My* will is separate from yours, and that I would have you do something that may cause you pain and suffering. This creates a split in your mind—a dichotomy to the truth that *My* Will is your Will and is the movement of *My* Love. We are One." It was there and then I shifted my prayer to, "My Will is Thy Will, Thy Will be done. We are One." Then the 'I' returned in all its radiance.

Any time you believe God's Will or purpose for you is in opposition to what you desire, this belief sets up a dichotomy in the mind which creates the effect of mental and emotional crucifixion from a fear that your desires are not God's Will for you. This belief implies you may be asked to let go of your dreams and desires. Ask yourself, "What is the source of my heart's desires?" If you have forgotten, go back and read the quote from *The Way to the Kingdom* in chapter one of this book. Your perception of what form those dreams should take, how they should look, or how they should manifest may not be clearly understood, but the fulfillment of what is at the core of your yearnings is already complete and simply awaits your full acceptance. When you claim your will to be the same as God's Will, you position yourself in acceptance, the second component of creative principle. When you call forth this one and only Will, you automatically surrender any false concepts you may have painted around the core of your heart's desire.

It is important for you to remember the definition of Love as understood from Gracemind. Love is the moving force, the *Will* of God drawing into your experience infinite possibilities of original design, and original design is always full of Grace and truth. Love is a component of your spiritual DNA. It is a given. Love expressing itself is the fulfillment of the Word. There is nothing within the Will of God that would have you suffer in any way. No, no, no—just not so, sweet One! God does not set you up for lessons to learn that cause you pain and suffering. God does not set you up for lessons, period! You set yourself up through the error beliefs you are tenaciously holding as your perceptions of Reality.

As you begin to use the Grace Prayer, you will see the words, *"Thy Will is my Will, Thy Will be done through me."* If used with the understanding presented here, they will awaken the depth of their truth in you, bridging the gap in your mind to an inclusive oneness, eliminating all questions, doubts, and fears that arise from the concept of two wills.

The prayer begins with the words, *"For Thee I thirst."* These words are fashioned after the recorded words in *John* 19:28, *"I thirst."* When you say these words, you are acknowledging your hunger and thirst to know God. You are intending your entire consciousness Godward. Then the words follow, *"Into Thy hands I commit my Spirit" (my soul, my body, my life, this problem—all unforgiven states).* This exemplifies the ultimate surrender required of any aspirant seeking enlightenment. The words are recorded in Luke 23:46 as, *"Father, into thy hands I commit my Spirit!"* I have simply extended them to be more inclusive. Surrendering through the process of accepting the alternative to what is desired to be released is the purest intention possible and the ultimate fear of the ego that wants to be in control. The ego will be crossed out in the surrendering and exist as the sense of separation no more.

The words *"Reveal that which is to be revealed. Heal that which is to be healed, that I may glorify You, God..."* express the ultimate desire for forgiveness—calling for the giving of/ revelation of truth for any error perceptions or beliefs that may be held in the conscious or subconscious levels of Mind. This is an interpretation of Jesus' words, *"Father, forgive them; for they know not what they do."* (Luke 23:34) These error perceptions are innocent, in and of themselves, knowing not what they do in mind, soul, and body. We are asking for them to be exchanged for truth, revealed, and healed.

Finally, Jesus is reported to have whispered, *"It is finished."* (John 19:30) You will find these words complete the prayer. They indicate to my mind that the prayer is complete, answered, finished. It is a done deal. Anything that is revealed is healed. All sense of separation held in my mind has been crossed out by the Grace of God. If I need to know what was causing this sense of separation and keeping me in a sense of crucifixion, I will know; if I don't need to know, it will simply be healed. The content of my mind will be transformed to reflect the resurrected, eternal life consciousness of Essence.

It has been my experience that the only things needed to be revealed are patterns of consciousness that reflect a sense of separation. The actual events that reflect these patterns are unimportant. Whatever is revealed that no longer serves you, take it back to the Grace prayer and surrender it. "Into Thy hands I commit my Spirit" (my soul, my body, my life—this need to be right, this need to control, this fear of annihilation, this pattern of belief/behavior, and so on). Get the idea?

The prayer is extremely powerful because of the intentions and purity of consciousness supporting it. It offers one-pointed vision and no-split desire. It evokes unconditional surrender with no investment in outcome or income. It places the conscious mind in a position of acceptance and trust as it looks to the superconscious/Gracemind for all wisdom and truth. It serves as an invitation to the Holy Spirit to begin a profound movement of revelation and healing. It is offered from the level of Mystic Mind and activates the awakening of Master Mind.

You may find what is revealed by the use of this prayer to be a bit overwhelming at first. Some students tell me they interject the words "lovingly and gently" after "reveal that which is to be revealed." It seems to soften the revelations and spread them out over longer periods of time so that the soul has more time for integration. I have even suggested that students stop using the Grace Prayer for a while if things are integrating too quickly. I used this prayer without sharing it with anyone for several years. Those years were the most transformative years of my spiritual experience. It is extremely effective if it becomes your last focus upon entering sleep or meditation. Here is the prayer:

Grace Prayer

For Thee I thirst.
Into Thy hands
I commit my Spirit,
(my soul, my body, my life,
this problem, all unforgiven states).
Thy Will is my Will.
Thy Will be done through me.
Heal me at depth.
Reveal that which is to be revealed.
Heal that which is to be healed,
that I may truly glorify You, God 'I' am,
living from the Essence of
Grace, now and forevermore,
into eternity's way!
It is finished!

During the day, as an instant positioner, I use a condensed version of this prayer which I have come to identify as my 'quick fix.' I simply affirm, "*I accept the Will of Grace, manifest now, in all, as all, and for all.*" This automatically positions my conscious mind to acceptance in stilled waiting. I am positioned to listening for inner wisdom, guidance, and instruction. I have found the truth within these words to be the movers of mountains without my doing one single thing. This is living *from* a consciousness of Grace.

There is another little prayer I have cherished for many years. It is an old Gaelic prayer, the author of which is unknown. It contains the same intention and context of the Grace Prayer. The words are incredibly magical when uttered from pure heart intention:

Gaelic Prayer

Oh ,Christ, Thou son of God,
My own eternal Self.
Live Thou Thy Life in me.
Do Thou Thy Will in me.
Be Thou made flesh in me.
I have no will but Thine,
I have no self but Thee.
Oh, Christ, Thou son of God,
My own eternal Self.

Intention is by far the most important element at the core of each one of these prayers. Each prayer reflects a heart yearning to know God as the Word made flesh as Christ consciousness. Each prayer vibrates at the level of the destiny encoded within. Once intended, these prayers establish a vibratory correlate of resonance as a magnetic attractor and environment of receptivity. Like will attract like. The law will be fulfilled by the Grace principles of abundance, acceptance, and freedom.

I have often offered a simple little formula for guaranteed answered prayer. It is based on the powers of intention, attention, and pretend-sion. *Intend* your mind and heart through these prayers. Place your *attention* upon the inner Spirit, waiting, watching, and listening. Then, as you go about your day, *pretend*, act as if it is already yours. Act as if it is complete and finished, for in truth it already is—otherwise, the desire could never have even been conceived. As you have learned, manifestations of all ideas, dreams, and heart desires are already fulfilled in and of themselves, similar to the analogy of the tomato plant already being fulfilled within its seed. So, go about your day acting as if it is already yours. This is a legitimate response to a legitimate way of prayer that proves the kingdom of heaven to be at hand. Acting as if and pretending bring out the little child in you. Make it fun, Beloved.

As with all prayers, it is important to remember that they are positions of focus which create an environment of receptivity in consciousness. They are *not* the *cause* of any effect. *Cause* rests explicitly in the already fulfilled idea/desire/seed of God. You are simply tilling the soil of consciousness to make it receptive for the seeds to grow.

There is one additional prayer I would offer as worthy of resting in Grace consciousness. It is called *The Prayer of the Chalice*. The author of this one is also unknown. It is fitting to place it last, for it serves as the magical cup that is offered up through Gracemind. This is a cup to be filled, not to be passed from you. It is the cup of the Holy Grail, the receptacle of the conscious and subconscious mind awaiting the wine of eternal life from the superconscious. Sit with it in your heart and drink from it often!

Prayer of the Chalice

Holy Spirit, to Thee I raise my whole
being—a vessel emptied of self.
Accept Lord, this my emptiness and
so fill me with Thy Light, Thy Love,
Thy Life, that these Thy precious
gifts may radiate through me and
overflow the chalice of my heart
into the hearts of all with whom
I come in contact with this
day—revealing unto
them the beauty of
Thy Joy,
and,
wholeness,
and
the
serenity
of
Thy Peace
which nothing can ever destroy.

Before the journey culminates in the fully awakened state
of Grace, there must be a willingness to release everything you
think you know and everything you perceive to be the definition
of who you are. This is the choice referenced in scripture as the
last enemy to be conquered, death. It is the choice to die to any
sense of self as you understand it. That choice is usually made
toward the end of Mystic Mind awakening. This prayer is a
perfect expression of that intention.

Chapter Eight

The Practice

Chapter 8

The Practice

I *am* the Practice in the practice, practicing.

As you continue to become more remembered in your Essence, you drink as though thirsty at a fountain of the eternal waters of truth, pouring not from without but from within. The holy energy which is contained within these living waters will set your awareness free and will free the generations of content held within the systems of mind, emotions, and body. These systems, once freed to receive the living eternal life waters of the Spirit, will be renewed as though a desert being fed with water from an unseen source.

Have you been asking yourself the question, "If I become fully enlightened, will I be the same as I am now, or will I be so completely foreign to myself that I cannot recognize who I am?" You are the Beloved of God, and within you there resides perfection of that idea. You will not remain the same except in your Essence. You will be without the sense of separation, and thus, free from all the fears that keep you in bondage. You will be lighthearted, and you will be compassionate—caring at a depth your heart has never felt before—a caring so compounded you will not be able to distinguish the one you care for as being separate from you. Your compassion will not contain within it the strains of stress, the strains of despair, and the strains of worry as before. Your caring will contain within it the vibrational *strains* (ancestry) of the Jesus idea of compassion, service, and love—extending yourself with great faith, joy, power, and strength unto the person before you. So, yes, you will be different, and, no, you will not recognize yourself, for you will not be the same individual—at least in awareness of that which is called Gracemind.

Reconciliations of the heart are taking place with many people, who, like you, desire to be reconciled with I Am. Each aspirant knows the power of reconciliation when it comes to

Grace awakening Essence. It has been revealed in my own awakening that in addition to prayer there are several practices which are of great value that generate accelerated reconciliations of the mind, emotions, and body. I offer you these practices through the words that were received from the voice of Essence in my prayer times. Practice of the truths contained within these words has changed me into a new creature in Christ, and I am humbly grateful and blessed.

Before you enter into these suggested practices, let me address an issue of importance. Some spiritual persuasions encourage you to become relatively non-doing—to spend hours and hours in prayer, meditation, days of silence, and similar practices. Some even advocate entering a monastery, moving to a high mountain, becoming a hermit, monk, or nun. There is absolutely nothing wrong in such practices as long as you are Divinely guided to do so. To retreat from the world as a means of escape, however, is not so enlightening. To everything there is a season, and to everything there is a balance. I don't usually give advice, but in this case I will. Seek balance. This is a created world, and the God you seek is both doing and being as you simultaneously. You are the extension of God, and as such you will find your greatest joy is experienced in *the stillness of the silence at the center of your creating*. To never experience the stillness of silence will drive you to madness and conjure up for you all sorts of unfavorable perceptions, conditions, and addictions. To never engage in doing, as in creativity, will stymie the flow of Life. To experience both doing and Being—stillness and activity simultaneously—is the ultimate bliss of one awakened in Gracemind.

In this world your Being finds itself drawn into much 'doing.' This is natural and healthy. When you take a few moments to be still, you find you are automatically drawn inward into the Essence of stillness. This is also natural. The eternal 'I' is at the center of both being and doing. This is known as the twofold path of one life—living in balance. To *be* without to *do* does not fulfill the laws of Being. To *do* without to *be* does not exist. Note the 'I' at the center of the words *Being* and *Doing*

within the circle. This 'I' at the center of both is the eternal
'I'. Read the circle round, and you will find a continuous flow
always returning to 'I' at the center.

Practice Number One: Don't Go There!

One afternoon as I sat meditating by a small lake in Dallas, TX, waiting, watching, and listening, I was given a visual. I have put this visual into practice many times when tempted to try my old way of healing memories etched in the soul. For many years it had been my understanding that it was necessary to dig deep into the subconscious, rooting out any false beliefs, fears, hurts, unforgiveness, etc. that I found rooted there. I was devoted to this process and dedicated to being responsible for all my issues and, therefore, responsible for healing them. Once I found any 'stuff,' my method of dealing with it was to sprinkle it with a few denials and saturate it with affirmations, believing this was the way to change its identity. After all, was that not the way the 'stuff' got in? Had I not, on some level of awareness, affirmed an illusion through my lack of understanding and denied a truth? It made sense to my Metaphysical Mind awareness to 'fix' my stuff through this method.

This technique seemed to work at first, but years later I would realize this application had only sent those error beliefs into remission. I had placed my faith in the affirmations and denials as being the healing agents—not in the truth to which they pointed. This old practice was the equivalent of expecting a band aid to heal the wound it covers. Only Grace and truth heal the wounded soul through the infusion of Grace consciousness. From this position, conscious mind focused inward toward the superconscious does not mistakenly identify itself as the healing physician by prescribing affirmations and denials. This should be easy for you to recognize by now.

As I began to put the vision I received into practice, miracles began to happen without any conscious effort on my part, other than to follow instructions, accept, and be happy. The work was done through me without effort, question, strain, struggle, or exhaustive investigation. It has proven to be a prescription that cures, not one that puts dis-ease into remission.

Here is the message and vision given, and I encourage you to put it into practice. In a nutshell, it exemplifies the Essence of one living *from/as* Gracemind.

*"You have been given the Promised Land, a literal Garden of Eden in My sweet Earth. Contained within it is every tree and flower of life you can imagine. It consists of 144 thousand acres of beauty and abundance. Any good thing your precious heart can conceive is there for your **acceptance**. Walk and live ye herein. The home of your dreams, the city of your greatest imagining, and the fulfillment of My design and desires written in your heart abide there. If you would truly glorify Me, please accept this as My gift to you, which, in My relationship to you, is My gift unto Myself.*

*There is one small area, however, within this 144 thousand acres that you are forbidden to enter. At the back of this property is 66 acres filled with the roaring memories of your fears, doubts, resentments, prejudices, and even-exchange ideas your soul has accumulated along the journey of awakening to my Grace-full Promised Land of consciousness. **DON'T GO THERE!** For to enter these 66 acres will make My gift of the Promised Land disappear from your view.*

There will be times you will be tempted to enter by the nature of your curiosity and need to know, but you must NOT! There is a key, however, that will empower you to make this choice and ultimately transform these 66 acres. Every time you are drawn near it, see this acreage as a radiating sphere of Light, and, in your Mind, which is an inheritance of My Mind, know this Light is and always has been the Light which guided you into My glorious kingdom on Earth. Let these 66 acres rest in peace, thus the lion and the lamb in you lie together, becoming one Light of My Peace, Love, and Joy. Then your world will be the garden of your soul as My Grace journeys you throughout eternal life."

Work with this visual, Beloved. Let it grow a Garden of
Paradise in you. You will be richly rewarded and save yourself
lifetimes of work in trying to create a weed-less garden equal to
this.

Practice Number Two: High Thought

The practice of high thought aligned with the truth
contained within Essence is paramount in spiritual awakening.
This is thought aligned with solution, not with problem. In
thought you must identify only with Essence, for herein abides
your freedom and your abundance. The voice of Essence speaks
to this idea:

> *If you bring a program of thought, or heart's desire to
> the present moment experience of Reality in which you
> live on a daily basis, this thought should be high—high
> and filled with the idea of eternal life and joy. Carried
> forth in your mind, this energy of Light in alignment
> with the high idea or heart's desire, will bring unto
> you an equivalent of the same. Master teachers have
> all understood this great truth—that according to
> the will of the mind is the life in front of you. Glory
> is that which is the word, carried with faith, trust,
> love, and joy. And therefore, that word comes to pass,
> for it cannot do otherwise, according to the law. The
> wisdom of the eternal Son, gathered in the strength
> of the I Am, seeking now to make a greater world of
> Grace encourages each one of you to hold the highest
> ideal which comes to your mind. If you will do this and
> collectively gather in strength, that which is desired
> shall come to pass, and a new world shall beget itself
> in earth.*

Hold this ideal: (Essence continues …)

> *I am the Will of God,*
> *Open to the Will of God I am.*
> *I am the Love of God,*
> *Open to the Love of God I am.*
> *I am the Peace of God,*
> *Open to the Peace of God I am.*
> *I am the Joy of God,*
> *Open to the Joy of God I am.*

Eternal living truths within these words will overflow gracious blessings from on High into the life's experience of each one of you. From the truth herein revealed, you will stretch forth your hand and partake of the eternal gifts of the table set before you in the earth—filled to capacity with your every heart's desire.

In addition, these high thoughts fulfill the first and greatest commandment to love the Lord your God with all your heart, your soul, and your mind. Such is the Grace of God and the fulfillment thereof. This is also the solution, the only solution to effecting a new world order of peace among all nations.

Practice Number Three:
Keep the Commandments of I Am

Let your heart accept the first and greatest commandment to love the Lord *your* God with all your heart, mind, and soul. Do this from the position of your awakened Master Mind which knows itself to be the extension of I Am. Practice the second commandment, like unto the first, to love your neighbor as your Self, for in truth you are One. Essence speaks about becoming the Master:

Becoming the Master

Can you stand before the mirror of yourself
And behold I Am?
Can you love I Am with all your heart, mind, and soul?
Can you accept that the love with which you love I Am is mine,
And mine is thine?
Can you believe you are the I Am of the eternal Christ,
And you carry within you the same power
As the master teacher, Jesus?
Can you allow this power to come forth
And to spread unto all that is,
Giving and shining the Light
Through all, in all, as all I Am?

I Am the Light of the world in all,
And I bring unto all a gift—the
'One' who stands before you in each individual.
It is I Am within them that comes into your Light,
And your Light I Am that comes into theirs.
Can you love them as your Self,
The I Am that I Am in them as you?

Can you, in every single moment,
Behold My Presence standing before you in all?
Can you, from the gift of your Spirit,
And the mind of your Spirit which knows this truth,
Find this truth as it looks out through your eyes?

Can you return unto those who take,
That which you would have yourself receive?
Can you be the giver and the bearer of good tidings to all,
No matter what they may do or say unto you?

Can you embrace all these things, My Beloved?
If you can, then you are the gift of My Grace in earth.

In another prayer session, the following message emerged. It speaks to the depth of love, faith, and trust that is the required practice of each of us as Master Mind awakens. I encourage you to read this often and make it a priority of focus.

The power of humble adoration for My presence in others
Will bring to you the greatest expansion
Of the gift of Grace in your heart.
And that one who stands before you,
Expressing the least amount of My Light,
To that one, if you can give this gift,
You shall become a Master in a short amount of time.

To the one who calls you by a name not so loved,
If you can find My voice in all that is spoken,
You shall become a Master in a short amount of time.
And to the one who bites the hand that feeds it,
And you be that hand which is feeding the little one,
Can you say to this one, I love you?
Then you shall become a Master in a short amount of time.

And to that which your eye at first does see no beauty rest,
Can you find it here in all you see? If so,
You shall become a Master in a short amount of time.

And some of you will be guided to take up your palette
And all that belongs to you and move away,
Or change locations, or occupations.
Can you do this in faith according to the
Instruction of the voice within your heart?
If you can, you shall become a Master in a short amount of time.

And can you lift your heart above the sadness of the earth
And the energy you feel when you rise?
Can you lift your mind and heart above this energy field,
And hold the joy of the Lord throughout the day?
If you can, you shall become a Master in a short amount of time.

Harmony is the gift of Grace,
And it runs through you as though a lifted bird
Singing its heart into the ' I Am.'
Harmony is the gift that unites all in harmony.
Can you hold the harmony of ' I Am'
All the day long—no matter what?
If you can, you know the result—
You shall become a Master in a short amount of time.

~ ~ ~

Practice Number Four:
Identify with I

This leads us into the fourth practice, which is to
identify yourself with the Cosmic Christ, the Divine I-dea for
humankind. This was the true message of Jesus. Jesus ushered
into the world, in every one of his teachings, the concept that
'I' is your Divine inheritance as the image and likeness of God.
'I' is the master key to understanding yourself as the Presence
of God individuated. Jesus' teachings identified with the
commandment to be still and know **I** am God. The 'I' of you *is*
God expressing.

There is nothing more powerful than bringing this
awareness to your everyday thinking, feeling, and interactions
within relationships. This can be done as you listen to others
speaking. Every time they speak the word, 'I,' let your mind
recognize they speak *of* their Essence *from* their Essence which
in turn *is your* Essence. Every time *you* use this sacred word,
pause just a fraction of a second, and in the emptiness of the
pause do as Christ would encourage you to do, "Remember
Me"—the 'I' of thee.

This is not as easy to do in your mind as it sounds on paper.
Try it. More than likely you won't be able to stay awake to the
intention more than a few seconds. You will, by the habit of
your mind, forget to pause to remember the I speaking *is* God.
Instead, you will launch into conversation from the same old
perception of self that perceives separation. And listen to your

words as you converse with others. You will be amazed at how
you speak of separateness. For instance, you may say: "I prayed
to God and asked *Him* to guide my way; God is *with* me always,
therefore I am not afraid; God *in* me can do all things." There is
nothing wrong with this way of speaking except that words like
to, with, and *in* when speaking of God place you in relationship.
To be in relationship requires two. Relationship implies
separation to your current way of thinking. You are awakening
to Gracemind in which there is no awareness of two, only One.
"He who has seen me has seen the Father." (John 14:9)

Now, here is a practice that will assist your mind in
breaking its habit of dualism. Instead of using the proper
English verb 'am' when you use the word 'I,' substitute the
grammatically incorrect but spiritually correct verb 'is.' Shifting
from first person to the transpersonal use of 'I' tweaks the
mind's habit and shatters the separated pattern because it is not a
logical pathway for the mind. Also, substitute the words *to, with*
and *am* with *'as.'* "As the presence of God, I does all things. I is
God and I is not afraid. I guides my way." Now this may cause
some of you to want to throw this book up against the wall, but
with willingness to embrace this practice, the merging that takes
place will be well worth your while.

My beloved husband, John, introduced this concept and
practice to my awareness. At first I thought it was a little far out
(to be honest, I thought it was just plane crazy), but as I joined
him, the depth of his wisdom, and the power of the practice
changed my life. If you begin such an exercise, I can promise
you it will change your life as well. It opens the single eye/I
of wisdom and understanding that integrates the 'I' of God
awareness with self. This can really be a fun practice when you
get your spouse or a friend to join you.

The Gospel According to John is the Book of Grace—the
Book of Love, and when you take the understanding of the 'I' as
being your Divine inheritance, the words that follow 'I' in the
teachings of Jesus will reveal the Essence of your Being and the
truth your Essence contains. I have gathered the 'I' teachings
of Jesus from *The Gospel According to John* and offer them

here as the living Word, "the Word made flesh" in every man, woman, and child. These words reveal the illusion of the sense of separation for what it is, nothing—no thing—and identify your mind, as was the mind of Jesus, with the Cosmic Christ, the eternal Son of God—the only begotten. Bring your eye to the 'I' in each sentence, and behold the Beloved of the 'I' of *you* and everyone, as Christ did when he spoke these holy words:

Words of Jesus
From the Gospel According to John (RSV)

Reference in *John RSV*

What do you seek?	1:38
Truly, truly, I say to you, you seek me.	6:26
Follow me.	1:43
I proceeded and came forth from God.	8:41
What I say, therefore,	
I say as the Father has bidden me.	12:50
I who speak to you am He.	4:26
I have come in my Father's name.	5:43
I know him for I come from him,	
and he sent me ...	7:29
I know my own, and my own	
know me, as the Father	
knows me, and I know the Father ...	10:14
... understand that the Father is in me,	
and I am in the Father.	10:38
Believe me that I am	
in the Father	
the Father in me ...	14:11
I and my	
Father are one.	10:30
You search the scriptures,	
because you think that in them you	
have eternal life; and it is they that bear	
witness to me, yet you refuse to come	
to me that you may	
have life.	5:39-40

I am the light of the world; he who follows me
   will not walk in darkness, but will
      have the light of life.   8:12
         I have come as light into the world,
         that whoever believes in me
            may not remain in darkness.   12:46

I have food to eat of which you do not know.   4:32
   Do not labor for the food which perishes,
      but for the food which endures to eternal life.   6:27
         I am the bread of life; he who comes
         to me shall not hunger,
         and he who believes in me
            shall never thirst.   6:35
            If anyone eats of this bread,
               he will live for ever ...   6:51

Is it not written in your law, I said you are gods? 10:35
   And I, when I am lifted up from the earth,
      will draw all men to myself.   12:33
         Will you lay down your life for me? 13:38

I am the way, and the truth, and the life;
   no one comes to the Father, but by me.
      If you had known me, you would have
      known my Father also; ...   14:6
         Have I been with you so long,
         and yet you do not know me ...? 14:9

I go to prepare a place for you ...
   And when I go and prepare a place for you,
      I will come again and will take you to myself,
      that where I am you may be also.
         And you know the way
         where I am going.   14:2-4
            I will not leave you desolate;
               I will come to you.   14:18

In that day you will know that I am in my Father,
    and you in me, and I in you.   14:20
        Abide in me, and I in you. As the branch cannot
           bear fruit by itself, unless it abides in the vine,
             neither can you, unless you abide in me.
                I am the vine, you are the branches.
                   He who abides in me, and I in him,
                      he it is that bears much fruit,
                        for apart from me you
                          can do nothing.   15:4-5

If you abide in me, and my words abide in you, ask
    whatever you will, and it shall be done for you. By this
        my Father is glorified, that you bear much fruit. 15:7-8
           Truly, truly I say to you, if you ask anything
             of the Father, he will give it to you in
                my name. Hitherto you have asked
                   nothing in my name; ask, and you
                     will receive, that your
                        joy may be full.   16:23-24

Whatever you ask in my name, I will do it,
    that the Father may be glorified in the
        Son; if you ask anything in my name,
        I will do it.   12:13
           You did not choose me, but I chose
             you and appointed you that
               you should go and bear fruit
                and that your fruit should
                abide; so that whatever
                  you ask the Father in my
                   name, he may give
                     it to you.   15:16

Truly, truly, I say to you, he who believes in me
    will also do the works that I do;

and greater works than these will he do ...   14:12
These things I have spoken to you,
that my joy may be in you,
and that your joy may be full.   15:11

I have yet many things to say to you, but you cannot
bear them now. When the Spirit of truth comes, he
will guide you into all the truth; for he will not
speak on his own authority, but whatever he
hears he will speak, and he will declare to
you the things that are to come. ...he will
take what is mine and declare it to you.
All that the Father has is mine;
heretofore I said that he will take
what is mine and
declare it to you.   16:12-15

I will make it known, that the love with which thou
hast loved me may be in them, and
I in them.   17:26
I in them and thou in me, that they may
become perfectly one, so that the world
may know that thou hast sent me and
hast loved them even as thou hast
loved me.   17:23
As the Father has loved me,
so have I loved you; abide
in my love.   15:9
This I command you,
to love one another. 15:17

In the world you have tribulation; but be of good cheer,
I have overcome the world.   16:33
Peace I leave with you; my peace I give to you;
not as the world gives do I give to you.
Let not your hearts be troubled, neither
let them be afraid.   14:28

	Peace be with you.	20:19
	Peace be with you.	20:21
	Peace be with you.	20:26

Whom do you seek?		18:4
Whom do you seek?		20:15
Follow me.		21:19
Follow me.		21:22

Promises are kept according to promises kept. I *is* the I Am, the Essence, the Grace of God you are. This is the promise kept at the core of your Being. Make a promise to remember your true Self—the I that is God, the Essence, Grace, to be the way, the truth, and the life, as did Christ. Be *that*—whatever it takes. Let this Essence be unfolded, trusting that within it is all you desire and more. When you remember this promise, promises within Grace's keeping are fulfilled, thus all promises are kept according to promises kept.

Practice Number 5: Become the Observer

Here is a practice that is becoming very popular in the Age of Grace. Become the observer of all thought, feeling, action, and most of all, Essence—the '*One*' practicing. Bring a stilled mind to the eternal always of present moment activity. Stillness is the highest frequency of consciousness in this plane of existence. In stilled awareness any content of mind vibrating at a level less than the highest frequency of the eternal 'I' is automatically absorbed by the energy of peace which is the matrix of stillness. The more you practice stilled observation, the more the content of your mind will fall into Gracemind, uncontrollably, and will be consumed by it. "Be *still* and know, 'I' am God." Make stillness a habit of your mind, and one day, when you lest expect it, you will know the '*One*' you are looking for is the '*One*' who is looking. In the search 'I' will find itself to be the eye of the I and the I to be the eye. My husband, John says it this way, "That which is sought is that which is seeking."

This realization activates a release that draws the body, emotions, and mind into harmonic flow. This harmonic flow of energy becomes the vibrational frequency which triggers an opening, drawing you, the aspirant, into communion with the All of God Mind. Mind then becomes the portal through which consciousness opens to reveal the unified field of oneness. This experience automatically shifts the journey from an outward or inward *search*, to *fusion* in awareness with the eternal God Self you have always been. In the twinkling of the 'I' of the Divine, fusion of awareness takes place in consciousness, merging the totality of your masculine and feminine nature which contains the consciousness of the All.

In the fully awakened state, you, as you have known yourself in the past, do not exist as a separate identity; you exist as a unique expression of God Essence. In this awareness it is as impossible for you to perceive a sense of separation as it formerly was for you to perceive unity. God awakens itself as your realization of the All. Duality is no longer your frame of reference, therefore, all illusory content of mind disappears, leaving only flowering Essence embracing the butterfly within. *"The flower invites the butterfly with no-mind; the butterfly visits the flower with no-mind."* Ryokan

Practice No. 6: Trading Spaces

Grace Awakening can be as simple as adjusting binoculars in order to bring an object into clear focus. A slight shift draws what seems to be far away, up close and personal. In the human condition you have identified with what is being viewed instead of the One viewing. A slight shift from the eye to I in the viewing of all life is a powerful movement that clarifies the focus of awareness. This shifts the consciousness of the observer from identifying *with* the observed to I-dentifying *from* the Essence *of* the observed.

Now, here is a subtle but major realignment suggestion. If you would intensify your understanding of exactly 'what' this I is, you would be able to make a major shift of consciousness aligned with your Divinity. Instead of asking yourself 'who am I' or 'who is this I that is observing,' ask 'what' is this I that is observing? What is the I of you? The answers you will receive as to 'what' this I is will begin to move you from identifying with 'what' is being observed to the 'what' that is observing.

Begin this practice by asking, 'what' is God? You will probably automatically respond with words such as life, consciousness, peace, love, joy, mind, idea, expression, energy, beauty, and so on. In your mind's current position, which feels separation, these descriptives present themselves as the observable to which you have given meaning. Now, ask yourself, 'what' is life? It will be very hard for you to clearly define life, but you may say you can feel it. Good. Every time you feel life, the Divine of you has been experienced. 'What' is peace? Your descriptives will probably describe what it feels like to *be* peaceful instead of describing peace. When you feel peaceful, this is the *experience* of the eternal Essence of yourself as Peace. What is 'love'? Well, this one has been a challenge for even the most prolific writers. Why? Because it simply can't be defined. It can only be expressed or experienced in order to convey its definition. What is 'beauty?' You will describe the beautiful. You will never be able to describe beauty, but you will forever be able to express and experience it.

Now here is the ultimate practice that will quantum Grace awakening. Bring your awareness to 'what' is being observed in your practice of being here now. As you observe whatever is the experience of the moment, instead of allowing the mind to categorize or identify the 'what' that is happening, allow the mind to *fall* as softly as a feather into the 'what' of the 'that' as the 'you' that is observing the 'what.' In other words, *become* the *that* of the *what* that gives rise to the capacity to grasp the moment's experience. This will give you an awareness of what it is like to be the song of the bird, the wind beneath its wings, the sun of the light of day, the beauty of the blossom of the flower, the fragrance of the rose—the Essence of the God you are!

My beloved assistant, Angel Gates had been working with this practice for some time when one day she fell totally and completely into the Essence of her Being. I asked her to etch that experience into memory more deeply by writing it down. Here is what she wrote:

"I began a practice several months ago of stretching after my morning exercise routine, where I would hold a stretch and think, 'I am flexible.' One day, as I held a stretch, something shifted in me; instead of affirming my desired state of flexibility, I heard the words, '*Be* flexibility,' and I began to experience myself *BEING* the actual quality of flexibility. This was far beyond any physical feeling of my body being more flexible; it came from a much deeper understanding of myself actually being all that is. I was fully present in experiencing the 'I' knowing itself as the quality of flexibility. I noticed that the more I relaxed into this peace-full state, the more flexible my physical body became. I began to integrate this into my daily practice of stretching. Each day, in order to experience the shift again, I began with the affirmation, 'I am flexible.' Then, as I held each stretch, I would think, 'OK, now *BE* flexibility,' and this would instantly take me into the shift.

Recently, as I was reading from the *Way to the Kingdom* about 'desire and its accomplishment being one and the same thing,' and reflecting on the idea of acceptance, I closed my eyes and thought, 'OK, now *BE* acceptance.' As I began to actually *feel* myself *as* the quality of acceptance, I was enveloped in an indescribable sense of immense peace and complete bliss. I felt electric as I let this awesome energy flow from and throughout my entire Being.

The shift in my perception of these attributes (flexibility, acceptance) from being *in* me to being *as* me has become a powerful tool in my process of awakening, and I have begun to use this practice with other attributes such as love, happiness, peace, etc."

Thanks Angel, you have expressed the power of this practice beautifully.

Awakening, Beloved, is simply that. Becoming awake to what already is. Much like awakening from a long night's sleep that held you in illusory dreaming, you now awaken from the sleep of your soul that held you in the dark night's dream of separation. You are acceptance vs. being what you accept. You are flexibility, therefore, you are flexible. You are understanding itself, therefore, you can understand all things. All of these attributes are your God Self. You are the Love of God giving and receiving love; you are the Life of God living from Life as infinite possibilities of life expressing; you are the Peace of God expressing and experiencing peaceful moments and situations; you are the Beauty of God experiencing ineffable beauty; the Joy of God experiencing myriad opportunities for happiness; the Will of God expressing the purpose of your individuated expression of your Divine Creator. If you are having some difficulty identifying yourself *as* these qualities of God Essence, remember this: you are not the *All of* God, but **all you are is God**. You are the created of the Creator, image and likeness. These realized truths will humble you beyond measure. Welcome home, Beloved. You as God is One.

Now, before I leave you with this practice, I would offer you this I-dea for your contemplation. Would it be possible for you to experience any expression of love if you were not already that? No. The Love you are is the 'what' that is capable of recognizing love expressed. How could you ever experience the multitudinous expressions of Love's possibilities if you were not already *that* Love? How could you possibly *feel* the love expressed, for instance, in your favorite movie *about* love? If you were not already Love, you would be incapable of knowing and feeling love expressed in any form relevant to the created world. The same is true of peace. If you were not already Peace, you could not possibly experience peace in the world of expression. When you read poetry, how would you ever be able to grasp the essence of the words of the poet's pen if you were not the *that* to which the pen describes? If you were not already beauty, beauty would not be recognizable by you. This brings new meaning to the phrase: "Beauty is in the eye of the beholder." Let us now elevate this profound truth to read: Beauty is in the **I** of the **Be**-holder!

What can you expect to gain from this practice? A life lived from the consciousness of Grace which promises: in Grace there

is no struggle; in Grace abundance flows freely; in Grace your
dreams are fulfilled; in Grace your destiny is revealed.

The more you practice the Presence, the more it will
practice you. In your awakened state of Grace you *are* the
known, the knowing, and the knower. You *are* the All and the
All of that of the All. You *are* the Eternal and the always, the
heart and the soul of existence, and the infinite I-deas within the
silence of the Silence from which existence emerges. You *are* the
Essence of the ocean of consciousness and the movement of the
waves of its Love. You *are* the peace of Peace, the love of Love,
and the joy of Joy. In Grace your physical being is moved, not
by self-willed action as before, but by the energy of Spirit. Your
voice speaks from the depths of the unknown as your conscious
mind is positioned as a spectator. You hunger and thirst no more,
for you are fed to fulfilling from your own endless Source. You
no longer practice the Presence for the Presence practices you.

Surrender is left behind in the cocoon of time, for you
are remembered as *that* to which you willingly I-dentified and
accepted yourself as the Grace of God. You are no longer driven
by a quenchless search—you are the soft, sweet fountain of the
eternal morning. You are the mountain and the valley, the sun
and the shadow, the awake and the asleep, the work and the
worker, the dream, the dreamer and the dreaming of Life. You
are Life itself as the eternal unfolding. You are empty of the need
for mission, goal, and journey. You are the open arms of God
accepting the All that is. Peace, Love, and Joy claim you as their
own, and you are the boundless Self, the butterfly of 'I' set free
to soar in the kingdoms of God. You are the hourglass of time
filled with Eternity. You are a tapestry of Light, the Essence of
the Divine, unfolding its unique and special gifts of seamless
Grace.

Section II

Essence Speaks

Essence Speaks ~

In Section One of this book, I began with the metamorphosis of the butterfly as a metaphor to illustrate the transformative awakening of consciousness through the activity of Grace.

Nothing is the same after this movement—you emerge as the totally free Spirit of the winged one you truly are. You are lifted above the consciousness in earth—you *are* the *truth* that has set you free. You remain in the world but not of it in the same way as before, and your conscious mind is continually fed from the purity of the Voice of God you are.

Section Two of this book, *Essence Speaks*, is a compilation of some of the teachings that have come forth from this fully awakened state of freedom within myself. My conscious mind still remains completely humbled by the Voice of my Essence speaking and teaching as me.

I do not remain in the vibration of these messages all the time, but I can say I am free and know myself to be a radiant individuated expression of the All, fulfilling my original design. My conscious mind is impulsed and taught by my superconscious. My mind and heart are filled with *That* which cannot be described. There is new wine in new wine skins offering the experience of a Grace-full life beyond imagining. This new wine is what has replaced the 'old content' that used to run my life. I am never without the awareness of guidance, abundance, peace, love, or joy. Life still offers trials and tribulation at times, but I now know myself as Essence and am not affected by them. Truth knows me to *be* what *it* is, and has set me free.

I now offer you a few of the messages of Essence speaking as the truth that points you in the direction of all truth and as the truth that is the core of the understanding about Grace Awakening Essence as expressed in Section One.

May the Source that is the Voice that already is your own,
be awakened and heard as you through these words, and may you
be set free in your expression of individuated Peace, Love, and
Joy. You are Divine, Beloved. May these words re-member you.

Linguistics of these words may sound strange; let the linguistics be rested in as it is rested in I Am. Listen with the heart instead of the mind, and allow what follows to flow. Let these words fall on those of you to whom I am called and realized in those of you who are ready.

Lovingly, you all seek to be expressed to a greater degree of love and be united at the level of the Christ's heart desire to be and to serve. Your wills connected empower you to accept what is already given, known as your desire in the Spirit of yourself as fulfilled. Welcome the Teacher within you as your own and that which you now understand to be your God—one and the same. Forever the Spirit moves itself, sweetly, softly, and silently, and herein is it expressed for all to understand as your own measure of life eternal.

Without exception each of you absorbing this message has been yearning to be used and served as the Love of God—and that you are! A greater and deeper acceptance of the level of the mind and the heart within Myself you call yourself, will bring unto you a deeper understanding and a greater expansion of this truth for which you yearn. You are My idea of Myself in this sweet realm called Earth, and I love what I have created with all of the heart from which I have created you.

The hallowed work in you is about the Love unfolding its light, truth, wisdom, and understanding. The Master within you recognizes itself, favoring the ideas of truth. Each of you has been called, and each has answered from My idea known to you as mind and heart. Your soul, gathering momentum and strength, moves forward. Luscious, rich, gracious, and generous, the heart of you rests in the opulence of its own idea of Self. Mind understands itself through Mind. Love beckons all into being, creating after the image and the likeness of the idea Mind embraces. From the core of the heart of God, the Love you are extends itself in earth and unfolds the wisdom teachings herein written from on High.

The unified field of positive and negative light completes a unit of Light (you) complete in itself having multiplied its energy field through wisdom teachings gained in each experience of life. As others have similarly created and experienced, they too have increased what is called the life expansion within the life which is I Am. Together, collectively, taking its units through its progressions of evolution and the expansions of the light frequency, you have what is called creation. Creation is a part and an aspect of all units of Light. The totality of creation is God Almighty, I Am. The nature of it is holy—the purity of it is Essence—the purpose of it is glory—gloried is I Am.

Lovingly, messages of this wisdom are received which are important to know. You are a member of the family of God, a unit of Light contributing to the whole, and each member goes forth and creates life according to what is impulsed from within by the within—connected, if you will, and a part of the experience of every family member. You generate and regenerate, create and experience the effects of the whole. You cannot escape the effects of the whole. It is impossible for you to be singled out and separate from thoughts, feelings, actions, and activities of the whole family of God. However, you can become an active participant in the collective unification and glorification of the family of God in your individualization. Thus, you affect all, including self.

Silken threads
The caterpillar spreads,
Not knowing why or how,
Enfolding a cocoon to itself.
Herein revealed the butterfly
In time, set free,
From silken threads enfolding thee.

Accept with open palm,
You would the butterfly,
Released from silken cocoon,
And watch Me fly,
As I in thee—Mastery.

And with the Mastery, responsibility,
Only to love,
And love alone.

Trust Me now, the Love I am you are,
To metamorphosis thee into Myself,
Remembered,
Set free from silken threads.

It is so important to understand this great truth, for herein lies the secret of humanity's fulfillment— the Divine Destiny and plan at work in all beings of Light. A being of Light is simply the Mind of God realized in its own sense of Self. If you take away the garment, clothing each individual's sense of self, there is only Self left. The totality of that equals you—not just the sense of you.

You have been called, and I have called you. All the yearning in your heart is the call being received. Hurry not in the earth, nor worry one iota in the mind. Useless energy is of no value. Love instead.

Fathered of the Father is My birth as you,
Given unto sweet Earth anew.
Again you've come returned,
Glorified by understanding the Love I am you are.
The journey now bears fruit for you.
So, Beloved, be still and enjoy.
Feel full, satisfied,
Knowing I am glorified,
My Beloved One.

Let us understand that what is in ideas of 'willed consciousness' seeks to find a resting place so that the Will of God alone can make itself known to you, child of Light. This Will of God, which is forever impressing itself for more importance to your conscious mind, is the final key or, if you will, mastery which must be rendered unto full expression in all.

The Love of God moves gently, so center yourself in the gloried idea of Love, and allow it to move you into wisdom. Wisdom teaches that long ago, far, far away in your concept of time, you were a child. Now you are an adult, matured, if you will, through spaces of experiences in this world and beyond. You are now gathered in the earth to proclaim, 'I am the Will of God and the consciousness therein.' You have spent many hours in rivers of generations past—streams, if you will, of consciousness evolving and revolving.

Hold the idea of simple abundance, gracious giving, and multitudes of information coming through. Let each idea given in a moment fill all space in your mind. As you allow it to fill all space, be with it constantly until whatever idea enters to take its place.

Let not your mind wander to future time, but keep a listening mind. Recognize that in each moment you have eternity and the gifts of God seeking to make themselves known.

Gravity is the closest idea that can be used to help you understand your footage in the sojourn of earth. There is a force that holds you in the Earth, as there is a force that holds you on the Earth. It is the life-force of generations past, present, and future in the eternal Always. Your experience is drawn by what is called your God I Am within— your Original Design. The force field then is what controls and enables. If you do not resist the force field, then by its nature it will keep you in and on the plane of existence which is suited for your evolution.

Gravity has a tendency to pull you down. That is why it is important to lift in the heart, above the crown, the halo or Light of God. This halo is not bound by gravity, but is pulled in a spiraling upward sphere by the heart of the eternal God in which you are being drawn to return to the cosmic I Am—remembered. This force field is much more powerful than the field of gravity in the earth and the gravity of consciousness that pulls you into past memory.

Multiply your wisdom through wisdom. Wisdom must be allowed. It is not manufactured from an idea or thought, but from an I-dea in My Mind. You are the wisdom of God I am, be still and know. Wisdom forever expands to teach of itself what is within itself given in each being of Light.

Wisdom is about understanding that it is wisdom that teaches wisdom, and wisdom gathers with it only what it is revealing—what is known—not what is to be perceived in your mind, but what is known. Be assured that as you seek to have wisdom revealed, it is I, the Love of God as you, who seeks to assist Myself in enfolding and unfolding, for you and others, that which I am.

These teachings raise the vibrational frequency of the Mind and, though this may seem confusing, they stretch Myself or My Mind so I may be more contained within Myself remembered or allowed. Never before have I been able to reveal Myself in such a way, for never before have I awakened as willing hearts and minds ready for equalization and emancipation.

The Will of God, which you have sought for so long, is the key to unlocking and revealing the Will to be the highest element of My Essence contained within that which is the nature of who you are.

Do you understand geometry and how it carries within it dimensional ideas? When you understand geometry as dimensional ideas, then you begin to understand eternal life as dimensional existences of Self, resting in I Am Eternal. You are making shifts in memory in order to abide in the space that can contain the geometry, if you will, the multidimensional dimensions within yourself.

Passages will come with frequencies of memory returning you to the one Love of God. Holograms of your own state will present themselves to you daily as you frequent the Earth in your experiences. And every time you take a leap of faith, you are spiraling, spinning, and propelling your own motion toward the summit which will give you a view of what you have spun through or mastered. Each evolutionary spiral into a new experience of life gives to the giver a blessing and empowers you with more creative ability. The holy Light of God is you.

You must learn to step over, if you will, to change modalities, to adjust frequencies, to refocus. That is why releasing the past is imperative. It is imperative to be able to release the past, for future memory cannot awaken in understanding or experience with past contagions.

Let this be your intention and your truth:

> *I will to will the Will of God, paramount.*
> *I am the Will to will I Am.*
> *I hold Myself—Myself holds me.*
> *I generate eternity.*
> *My beacons of Light powered by I Am,*
> *Create and are forever multiplied,*
> *And the Master teacher within me,*
> *Which is called to itself*
> *To know more of I Am that I Am*
> *Is forever glorified!*

Nature,—trust this idea, nature. She is a Being of great magnitude filled with the knowingness of my Will. Resilient, she is the epitome of trust and forgiveness. Thus, your soul seeks and covets what is nature's experience, for it teaches a greater nature of what is to be known within the nature of God as you. When you resist My Presence, you resist what is called your own nature. This is all that causes pain, and this alone. You never ever see nature resist itself. Watch carefully every aspect of nature. You will not be able to find resistance. It knows not of it.

The collective consciousness of humanity has a great gift, and that gift is called the ability to resist. This is an advancement of the element of awareness which nature does not contain. It is a gift to be given by the giver, which you are, to the experience of life in creation when appropriate. To create new life, you must have the gifted gift of resistance; however, to use it against the nature of who you are is truly in error. This resistance is caused by what you call willful mind. Yet, the paradox is, without will-full mind you would not have the gift of creation, for you must have the power to will in order to create.

Herein is a great mystical secret known only by the sages of ages. That which is the gift is also that which is the sword, and it must be treasured for the life it can give and disassemble—it must be respected. It is, therefore, imperative to know how to resist non-resistance and to never resist the nature of God you are. You must allow the free flow of the life-force, and when it flows freely to have you resist, then you use the sword with wisdom.

The Master teacher, Jesus, taught from the center which has perfect circular vision, knowing when to resist and when to use non-resistance. When you reach that point of circular vision, you, too, will know when to hold and when to fold. You will know when to speak, when to be silent. You will know when to move and when to stand still. You will know when to stand for what you believe, with strength and voice, and when to be quiet, completely at rest—knowing the truth. You will know when to be gentle and when to be strong. Only in circular vision, with non-resistance to the force that sees through the eyes that behold, will you be able to create in the manner which you, as a programmed creator, were created to express.

You must practice what you understand to be listening. When you practice listening and allowing what is heard or impulsed to move you, you will begin to feel this circular vision guide you to do or not to do. As you follow the impulse with no resistance, you will understand this teaching. Until then, it is just a perception in the mind, an ideal to be understood in the future. It must become your reality in the present moment so you can express as all you were created to express and assist the world in moving into the next dimension of expression—creating a new, according to what is the circular vision within I Am.

Bring this focus to your awareness many times a day: I seek to be the Will of God I am. This idea will take on many levels of understanding, and the intention will intensify itself by the progression of energy modulations from the thought pattern, which in turn, will increase your desire to be all it contains.

Your willed imaginations bring about the frequencies necessary to implement change. As you move into the times of change for the work ahead, you are definitely going to be patterning your life more each day after Jesus the Master, for his truth is the Will you came to serve of all I am. Let this Will, gathered in the stories of Christ, fill your household of consciousness as you seek to remember and forget. It is not an easy time in the earth, as forgetting and remembering (seemingly opposed ideas) seek to occupy the same space. My Will resides as the consciousness of eternal life, and when this willed idea of My Will is brought to the surface of the conscious level of memory, all that has forgotten My Will disappears. If you abide in the Christ by taking the thought, 'I will to will the Will of God I am,' then, this idea will multiply and bring itself to completion.

Do not be dismayed at the frequencies or the failures to immediately bring about the future desired state in I Am. But, seek with faith, trust, and clarity—the gift—by knowing that at the center of the impulse for the gift is the Light—focused upon its intention, willed by itself, generated within you many eons ago. Do not be surprised if in the days to come you feel this Light, much like you would something very small beginning to grow very large within. As this begins to happen within your soul, the membranes, or veils of the soul which do not serve you, will split wide open and fall away.

Let your time be spent with the Lord as much as possible in memory, attuned to the idea of present moment God I am. Hold your frequencies of resistance to this idea gently, gently. They will come, they will come, and they will come; but gently bring your mind back to the idea, I am the Will of God I Am. I am the Will of God I am.

Let penetrating fields of light move as they will in you—move. Let them move, and let everything come to pass. Speak your truth. Accept your energy. Feel your emotions without attachment—watch!

The whole truth, which has sought to express itself in you, is going to be revealed, slowly. Memories of generations past will be surfacing. Likelihoods of encounters with reincarnated friends are getting smaller and smaller, for karma is coming to a close, and what is called future memory or Ezekiel consciousness is awakening at the River Jordan's edge, so to speak. The memories of so called sojourns of the past, carried like a satchel on your back, will be lost. They cannot survive in the kingdom of God for there is nothing to sustain them.

The holy Light of God, which is in all, seeks to make a kaleidoscope of consciousness so that each unit of Light can bring to its focus the parameters of consciousness entwined and enfolded in every state of existence from within—naturally, holding Light. Spectrums before you will appear, and the Love of God, which penetrates into each idea of thought, will make itself fully known.

Registrations from on High will bless you with the gift of Light. As you experience this Light, each of you will have a different experience of what that energy feels like. Movement, stirrings, penetrations into the heart fields of remembrance, are felt as love, joy, pain, and sorrow. Be not afraid, for as the coming of the Christ was promised of old, so it is with you now. Each of you will have your own personal experience of blessings, gifts of Grace, and light which God empowers by the Holy Spirit to bring you ideas of joy. Be assured God is making itself remembered as you.

*Making a difference is simply making a
change. And when they are viewed as equal, it
shall be done by the choice you make. Energy
always reveals the magnitude of its equal in return.
So choose Love, the highest frequency, that I may
be made known to Myself you are. Love Me now,
as I love you loving Me—this is one and the same,
making a difference by making a change.*

*Strangely enough, change does not agree with
those who seek the Will of God, for to change
means to adjust many things and to trust there is
a power bringing greater fruit from shifting. It is
easy to trust as you stand beneath the tree bearing
fruit of the past service. Be willing to move beyond
your sown garden into the field of Grace sown by
God, to which you are One, revealing new fruit,
new fields of light, and new dimensions of service.*

In this Word is contained the eternal life, the elixir that has been sought for generations past. You are that of which these words speak—it cannot be found, but it will be remembered. To seek with the intention to remember all that I am will bring unto you the gift of 3-D vision.

You stand as soldiers before the I Am, which gathers with you an army of assistance from on High, and a promise by which to master and conquer. You are given all that you need for protection, but you may walk through what is called the valley of the shadow. In the valley of the shadow you will know the shadow as the gift. For here, as you see the shadow for what it is, that which gives dimension to every world, you will be able to rise above. Before, all you could see was the shadow. Now you will see the three dimensions as they are revealed to thee. You are the Beloved. Create your gift. Hold Love.

Each of you has the gift of Spirit, and the gift of Spirit is unique to each one, yet it complements the Spirit in all. As these gifts unfold into the light of remembered union and creation, what you create from the aspect of knowing this truth will be beyond your grasp to entertain at this time.

*Have you ever questioned in the past? Of
course, you have. Have you ever doubted in the
past? Of course. The doubt is what has brought
you to a new point of awareness or place to
see a new perspective of the aspect of whatever
truth you questioned. And so now, as you enter
into these times, do not expect that aspect of
conscious expansion to be much different. The only
difference will be a center point of knowing that
as you question, whatever the question may be,
it is impulsed by the Source to reveal more of the
Source as the answer.*

*No more questioning or wondering from a state
of frustration, but a questioning and a wondering
from excitement and joy, knowing that the
questioning and the wondering is what brings forth
what must be understood in order to have a greater
capacity for creation in God.*

To the one being called, I am the answer within seeking understanding to be given and received. Questions of the mind bring before the alter of the Presence which now is resting as the Voice in you, and herein lay the question before the Voice to be spoken in answered form, remembering that it is I that bring the question, therefore, I fulfill the answer. And the mustard seeds begin to germinate as realized information and wisdom from on High.

\

You are attracting light because you are Light. In this attraction, you become more unified, always, and when the mind cooperates with the natural Light force at the center of all life which you are, bringing its focus into alignment with the Essence of being that exists in you at all time, then you begin to absorb and attract light at frequency levels beyond your current measure. The Light then is free by what is called no interference from the mind. It is free to take within itself what is given of the Light called wisdom, love, understanding, and transformation of the soul.

Passion is a commodity of the heart and the mind brought together in a focus of great willed intention. As the mind sits in its stillness, waiting upon the Lord, Light entering by that intention fills the space of mind and heart with the gift of desire. Desire in you is the passion of God seeking, if you will, a mind/ heart, an instrument of Light such as yourself, which it can use to wield its desires into manifestation.

The gift which is seeking to be made known through you is what God would have you entertain as a blessing glorifying God's name. Those who do not interfere, but hold the gift as the joy or blessing given, already received—glorify God and the desire of the passionate heart of God Almighty to come into manifestation. Thus, we have heaven in the Earth.

Doubt, fear, and worry are disclaimers to the passion of God. These are the sins that keep the child in suffering and the Light from being recognized in order to bring forth its greatest glory, the passion of the Lord.

Holy is the energy that seeks to make itself known through each of you. Open your minds and hearts to the gift. Let the desires of your heart be recognized as the passion of God to fulfill its nature through you as you. It is I Am One.

Lift your hearts to a place of total acceptance. When you can totally accept the desire, the manifestation is assured, for there is nothing left to interfere with it coming to pass. If you resist in any way—with doubt, fear, worry, anxiety, anger, resentment, or withholding, that which is the passion of God cannot manifest. The passion of God is always brought into manifestation by consent—I accept I Am—I rejoice in I Am—I peacefully move through life as the gift, giving itself as me.

Within the desire of your heart, My fountain of ideas seeks to manifest into this world which I create through Myself as you. My Will of the desire impulses the yearning in your heart, and the yearning impulses the desire to will the yearning forward. The yearning is the gift which impulses the manifestation of that which I came to serve— Myself in Earth through I Am you are, child of Love.

'I' is the presence of all life in existence and beyond, the Source from which all life emerges. I, the gift and the giver, and I, the giver and the gift, am you. Name and claim your heart's desire, for truly it is Mine, and speak the word: thank you, oh Lord I am You are. Enjoy—in joy.

A welcome mat is always an invitation to enter into My home, which you call your own. A yearning is the welcome mat to enter into the manifestation of My heart's desires as your own. Forever, and forever, and forever, and beyond what your mind understands as forever, am I the keeper of Myself you are, and the Source constantly returning unto Source.

Your joy and your laughter serve as the arising, the bubbles, if you will, floating in their own revelry as the Immaculate Conception of I as thee, oh My Beloved One. Let your joy and laughter be your gift to give unto Me. Forever am I lifted by the joy of the Spirit you are I am, and thus, I expand within Myself welcoming all into My home as your own—the Source of all desires fulfilled.

Master teachers, each of you, listen carefully. The gifts of Spirit you have sought to have fulfilled as Joy, Peace, Love, and a sense of oneness in God, are the passions of the Lord seeking to make itself known to itself in you that it is. Worry not, My child. Do not be afraid. Listen only with your I Am to the truth that seeks to bless itself as you. Let the words of the inner Voice speak loudly to your heart. They are easily discerned by the frequency of joy that is felt. That which is known is given. Holy be these words to you. Take them as a gift of Grace, and let not your eyes move away from this teaching until it has engaged the totality of your Being so that you are truly open to what you are.

The Master teacher within you knows this truth, and it will say, "Yes, I do understand." Help yourself by being very still and looking toward the gift of God's holy Light as yourself. You and you alone can know the truth, and it can only be revealed through that which is you.

Many will come to mirror yourself, but only you can feel and know that which is looking at you. You are the One you seek. You are the Light that is welcomed in God. You are the current Reality of all truth. You are the Beloved I Am.

Peeks of information will flow. Do not try to understand them all at once, but know when they enter into the mind to give you wisdom in the earth, they will always remain. They will be accessible to you through your stilled awareness. Focus often at the pineal gland. Keep the center of the Light there in holding patterns of still I am. Be not afraid to enter deeply into the cranium of consciousness, and be allowing to yourself in all thought that enters into this position of knowing.

Let not any thought become crystallized, but allow its free-flow as a river flowing in and as your awareness. Seek not to hold any vision other than I am the Will of God. Let, therefore, your heart be pure. Let your mind be single in its thought and feeling. Let each one of you claim the I Am Presence of Jesus Christ—that which is already given you, let it be known today. Take no thought less than:

I am the Will of God.
Blessed be I Am as me, for I am true.
I am all in all.
I am that which is I Am.

I believe in that which is faith,
For faith is given in the seed,
And I am trusting that which is the
Seed to know how to give forth
That which it contains.
For in that which is the desired given,
Is faith revealed.
And here the faith begins—
A Word made flesh.

*Focusing upon My ideas which fill your mind,
let them of themselves generate the future. Hold
these ideas as you would a small child cradled
in your arms. Let them find a safe place to rest,
and rest alone. Do not seek as you would to make
the child grow, for contained within the child is
the Life that grows itself. Allow the ideas, when
focused upon with love, to grow to their own
fullness and become the perfected ideas which
are contained as that which is held within your
arms in perfection–a child in innocent perfection,
complete! This practice is perfect to draw your
future design into maturity.*

*Lovingly, allow your dreams to rest safely in
your arms of Love, and hold these dreams close
knowing they are the gift of the Light given as you.
Seek not to make these dreams something more
or less than they are. Do this by allowing them
to simply unfold and grow of their own accord.
Nurture, protect, shelter, and embrace them. The
Will of God will bring them to completion and
fulfillment—to extend itself, they will be given.*

Promises are kept according to promises kept. These are the commitments in your heart to be I Am. Keep the promise within your heart to yourself—be the love of God—be that at all cost—it is the pearl of great price you seek.

Purifications of the heart are now in order,
As I, My promise kept,
Reveal Myself—extended,
As the sunlight moves across the Earth
From hidden clouds.

Rainbows, if you will,
Are now in store,
As storms have passed.
They are no more.
Be still and know My promise kept in you,
As that which your heart desires.

Captured in My will,
The light as rainbow's sun—
In you—My Love, I have just begun.

Guidance followed is Mine
To be filled with gifts
Received unto Myself is yours, My love.
Can you but see, 'tis I indeed.
Remember Me.

Jesus, Master teacher, gathered in us all
Promises kept.
I shall return unto Myself.
I bring remembering,
Remember Me.

Let your mind be rested. It is the most important lingering that can be entertained by you in a moment's time. If you can come to the understanding that listening as the stillness of silence is the only activity that is needed for your entire being to fill all moment in space, you will be gifted beyond measure in your ability to gift yourself with what you seek to receive.

With you abides all that is needed. My Joy rests within you as the smile rests within the newborn. My Essence rests within you as the fragrance rests in the rose. My Love rests within you as the beat within the heart of God I am you are, and My Peace rests within you as the stillness of stillness. Go in Peace, My Love, and be still. Be stilled by stillness in the stillness that you are, and you will know Me as I am.

Least ye be afraid to take no thought, rest in the stillness from which the thought emerges. Be stilled by the stillness I am you are, and herein you will see Me always, all ways. Infinite is infinite, and always eternal. Stilled awareness is the pinnacle of the infinite eternal position of Love to be remembered, so be still, and here I am received.

No thought, take it.
Let it take you,
And the difference will be amazing!

Allow what is held in your heart
To be reversed and realized.
'Tis I holding you
And you holding Me.
'Tis I in all you see!

As the hills in the mountains rise, so am I in you.
And in the valleys, 'tis I that walks through,
Remembering me,
Throughout eternity,
And all I see, herein again I am.

Valleys rest within the mountains,
And the mountains rest within the valleys.
One without the other cannot exist.
I rest within you, and you rest within Me.
One without the other does not exist.
Be in rest, Beloved.
Hurry not.

My Love in you is the hunger and the thirst. It is the gift already given to be remembered only, for it is already received. Let your hunger and your thirst be your joy, knowing I am seeking to reveal unto yourself as Me, all for which you hunger and you thirst.

My God, My God,
Thou hast given unto me—Myself,
And herein in the Earth do I find You.
I love Myself.
Myself loves me,
Companioned throughout eternity
The Love of God revealed.

Worlds within worlds, I am taken in the evolution. Jesus Christ, the Master teacher, to him I am equal to his love. That which is offered is the solution, for it is the keeper of the Light of God. Let not your heart be troubled. Neither let it be afraid, for I am the promise kept within you.

Vortexes of light spin, and spiraling motions swirl dervishly. Mind rotations are multiplied and simplified. The Light holding you is the Light you are holding, and it beholds the Light in all. I gift Myself in abundance, for abundance is My joy. In your joy, abundance receives itself, allowing Me, My joy, to be received from Myself you are.

Happiness returns the gift of holy light into a greater capacity for happiness. The gift at the center of this joy filled energy field gives new birth to new levels of awareness, allowing the current level of awareness to be drawn into the new level of awareness so that nothing is lost. As these measures of units complete their circular motions, spiraling expandedly, the Will of God increases its Grace, if you will, and all is blessed.

Remember this:
As to the mirror
Bring eye, the I in you each day.
Stand before the mirror's gaze,
And see Me there with single eye
Looking back at Myself.
Question not the why,
The where, the when.
Let not the word 'but' or 'if' gather
Strength within.
In the morning's light,
Stand before the mirror
And smile at Me,
And I will smile back at thee.

Rock yourself as a child in a cradle,
Allowing the rock to be known
As that which nurtures the soul—
My energy of Love.
Sit quietly, Love, and allow Me the rocking,
To be gifting Myself nurturing thee.
I am your cradle throughout the beyond of eternity.

Clipper ships sail the seas.
My wind is captured in their canopies.
Hallowed be My name
Written on their bow,
Proud and stately as they plow
Through My ocean I have created for them
To rest upon in their sailing winds.

And such it is, My precious One,
My soul, the sea within yourself,
Supports the you here in the Earth
Sailing through.
Allow My breath to be the wind
Within the sail of your soul
And carry you where I will.

I am the trust with which you are trusting—
The wind that blows as your breath,
And I will bring you home,
Unto Myself in every port I take you to.
Wherever you are, I am kept.

Fathoms deep is My soul to explore as the ocean—fathoms deep, endless, if you will. Fish you have never seen before—ideas, ideas. Swim freely as I swim and take you where I will to explore My endless sea, so the I, the eye of thee, may truly see One in thee I am.

I carpet Myself for your footage in the earth. Follow the carpet I have laid before you—always. It is followed simply by the realization that it is I that take the step, I that guide the step, I that am the step, and that which is stepped upon. We are One.

*The pathway in the forest is created by the
one that walks it, and I am the pathway and the
one that walks—you are that. The sun shines
because it knows nothing else but how to shine.
The bird sings, for it knows nothing else but how
to sing. The river flows, for it knows not how to do
anything less. And you, My Love, love because you
are Love.*

*Your love is what complements the song in
the bird, the flow in the river, the fragrance in
the rose, the light in the sun. Each of these are
complementary of the One I am you are. Feel the
song as does the note that carries it, and let this be
your assurance I am there.*

"If I give, I shall receive" contains within it a condition. And, in the pure, eternal life free flow of God's energy into life, there is no condition attached. It flows freely without condition. Contemplate this idea, "I seek to serve eternal life," understanding that eternal life is without condition or end. "I seek to serve eternal life." In this way, as every idea contained within your individuation of the Self of God is brought to the understanding of selflessness, you shall embark upon a new frequency of service which is totally unencumbered or limited in any way.

Sitting quietly as the sun rises each day, feel the Son rise in you, 'tis I. Let every morning be to you as sweet as the kiss of dew to the earth, and, thus, I am nourished. Linger often in the light and let it fall across your face remembering: "My heart's desire is to will to will the Love I am you are." Let this be the message that empowers you to serve.

*Each of you, looking at that which is aware
in the other one, find the gift of Grace in all,
and you will understand more of the unified field
which the mind of unified Love now brings you—a
time of knowing. Hold: "I Am the Presence of my
God. My God is the Presence I Am. I am willed to
understanding by that which I am and guaranteed
that which is the gift—what comes as that which is
given by I Am Love."*

Coming together in one understanding, the will to will love is your gift. And every time your smile sees itself as Mine, whether on your face or another that I keep, shall it be given in return, and I shall be blessed within Myself. Such is the will of My Love.

Wouldst thou be servant unto the served, serving that which serves all I am? Of course, you would. Thus, the heart is filled to fulfilling, serving that which is serving all—My Love. And in the earth as Christ walked in the children's way, on bended knee was he to them. So be it this day, My Love. Bend before the child within yourself and them, for here in innocence kept am I, eye to I. See Me there.

From the depth of the soul that seeks to know—here I am—Lord I be! And the movement in the earth of My Love extended through your hands, your feet, your eyes that see, 'tis I indeed. No more, no less, but all I am is yours, Beloved. Seek only Love's embrace embracing you. Thus, feel that which has before been felt as need—now your dreams come true. I love you.

I love the adoration
That gives of its own accord,
Impulsed by the Love I am you are.
Let this be to the altar
Of your heart each day—
Adoration of the Love you are, My Love.

I am the keeper of the flame
And the flame itself,
The breath of life as you.
Each breath I take as yours is Mine.
Remember Me in time.
Falcons fly free.
Such it is with the soul of thee,
My Love, My precious One in all.

Mercy is given through My smile as I beacon Love's joy through your own. My own comes forth in others. See Me there. I, the Beloved, am your Love that I seek not—but am, filtering through systems of belief, absorbing as I drift below and within. Communications are opening wide. Balconies of heart, as though Romeo to Juliet, lovingly entertain ideas of sweet, sweet holy union.

When you wish upon a star,
It makes not difference how far away the star.
The wish is captured by My Light,
Returned unto you, Beloved One,
For My delight.
Trust.

As to the trellis climbs the rose,
So do I climb
In the revelation of the mind
Which is Mine as yours,
And herein do I bloom.

Afterthoughts no more keep,
Allowing only that which is I Am to seep
Into your mind.
For herein I am kept.

And Love as seedlings sows the farmer,
So do I in you,
Every time the Love revealed
Expresses anew.

And I hold Myself
As the butterfly in freedom's name.
Lovingly now, I entertain
The love of God I Am.
And sweet hereafter is the same,
Written in My heart, remembering.

Beacons of joy as swans to the lake,
I rest upon the water—
The Source providing all I need
To stay afloat.

Mother Earth as Mother Goose
To loved ones in her keeping,
Keep I Myself in you.
Falcons fly free,
Over land and over sea.
Such is I as thee,
My Beloved One.

Joy in the morning sings the bird.
My joy sings you in silence yet unheard.
Be still and know.
As I, the Love of God I am,
Know Myself as you.
I love you. I am there.

Every tear brings salt to earth.
Allow them to be shed,
While remembering Me instead.
Holy be the idea: I am here in earth, and I accept.
Let this be your prayer, 'I accept.'
Nurtured, mothering, captured with Light,
And I was birthed overnight.
Into the manager of the heart of God, sweet Earth accepted me.
Wouldst thou not be the accepting One
Returning unto Me, My Love in revelry?

Feel yourself cradled as mother's arms to child.
Believe and rest awhile.
The life you are My nature keeps,
Cradled in the arms of Love.
A mother's keeper am I in you.
And I, the Love you are,
Shall be forevermore eternal
In the Love I am as true.

I begin again, A new day dawning,
Beginning in time.
Forget the past, and be as child
To nursery rhyme.

I impulse unto Myself, remembering
That which you have called is Mine,
And herein hear Me now,
I give all I am in time—as you.
Question not how or who.
Just believe I am you.

Practice the Presence. How simple can it be?
For I practice what Is for all eternity.

Gather others with you, My Love.
With your smile, and love, and gaze, see Me,
And all will know that I am thee,
And all are Me.

Walk in the footsteps of your own,
With a mind that sees and knows:
God is home in me.

Be not afraid, and take no thought,
As the Master Christ instructed thee,
And Peace shall be your own,
Enfolded in the blanket
Of the Love I am you are.
Herein wisdom teaches from its own,
And you are empowered from on High.

As the morning do I open eyes in each of you.
Be still with gaze and gaze alone—
No words to speak,
And I shall whisper all words
The treasury of your heart doth keep.
Be still.

And as the river runs in stillness,
Let this be known in you.
I love where 'ere I'm kept,
And I am kept in you,
As morning in the dew.

*My Kingdoms come in each and every One
To which is Love I keep within Myself.
Creation's glory is My own,
And when revealed, accepted herein,
The Mind I sent Myself in all,
To it shall I be known.*

*My Love you are, My precious One.
My Love you are I am,
And as the shepherd to the sheep
And especially to the Lamb
Of God, I am.*

Mustard seeds,
So tiny in the soil I plant Myself.
Into a mighty tree I grow.
Humbled, as My branches bend,
Resisting not the wind,
Be I to know.

Love returns as golden birds that migrate coming home—Love returns. It knows the way. It is the path of the soul seeded in the heart of the Winged One you are. With Love everlasting guiding your way, the heavens are yours to soar. The sunlight shines, revealing what is in store. My heaven is here. There is nothing more near than heaven here. I walk in it as you, and all it takes is a tiny seed to be revealed. You are that!

Trust this: Guaranteed is My contract written in your heart. The mustard seeds are sown in the guarantee, to be revealed is that which is not seen in the seed by the naked eye but contained, nevertheless, the miracle of the tree. And I am such a mustard seed as thee, Beloved One, yet to be revealed—the mighty tree of life, eternal, forever begotten of the only One I am. Mustard seeds planted long ago, lifetimes beyond this one, now bear fruit in Myself you are. For fertile soil have I received unto My own, keeping safe that which is written in My heart as yours. Welcome home, Beloved. Be loved by loving!

To single the eye is to become one
And accepting of all.
Let thine eye (I) be single.
Picture perfect with the eye (I) single.
Thus, 'I' am glorified.
And 'I' shall see Myself,
Heaven, deep inside the eye that sees
The 'I'.

*Listen carefully, for precious are the moments
in time to the instructions from on High of your
Self given unto you. They are Mine, and Mine
is thine, and all is seeking to manifest in time.
Furthered by the yearning to serve, this is a new
day dawning—incorporated and gathering, if you
will, all of the experience of yesterday. Be assured
it was not wasted. Ours is to love one another as
another loves us, and ours is to know the shepherd
and the sheep. Ours is to believe the only thing in
life worth living is love, and peace, and joy, and
the expression of the above. So let it be, My Love,
and peace shall enfold thee in the expression to the
revelry of that which heals and that which serves
peace, and love, and joy with great ease.*

Wisdom follows you as you follow wisdom and teaches from itself. Love follows you as you follow Love. And the Master within comes forth to proclaim as Christ, 'The day has come that I know Myself to be the Lord God I am, and thus, I glorify'.

Sculpture yourself,
Etched in the eyes of you,
As you look at Me
Looking back at you
In others eyes.
And herein find the glorified,
And call Me through.
'Come, My Beloved, I love you.'

Let this be your voice
Spoken silently within.
To everyone's eyes
Behold no sin.
Instead, Behold the Love of Me,
My I looking back at thee
In others eyes.

Love moves forward expanding as space in time. Prepare to be seeded with greater love to sow again. The call to love is the call I am you are. Accept now the Love I am you are, and herein is the majesty of Grace unfolding. Precious moments are these in this sweet Earth. Awake that which has slept, for slumbering keeps what is precious in My heart until the time is ready—like the sun shifting night into day, it is time!

Let all the Earth keep silent by accepting what is within and without, above and below—only Love. Further My Love—silence keep, as I in the fruit within the seed—silent lay in earth. Multitudes emerge from a tiny seed the silence keeps.

*I welcome One as My own
In the multitudes before Me.
Stand before Me now
In that which you see,
The multitudes of Me.*

You are My practice and My Presence.
You are My awake and My asleep.
The Love of God
In every moment do I keep
The promise written in your heart as Mine.

Walk in this truth with your heart held high,
As you look at Me eye to eye
in all you see.
Herein I Am believed.
My Wisdom recognizes its own,
My Love the same.
My Peace and Joy,
Hallowed be My name.

Frequencies blend, harmonized by My voice—
the music of the spheres, and I am moved in you to
movement's sake for My joy.

The whirling dervish spins as spin and spins
again, until s/he becomes one with that which is
within.

The tree moves with the wind in its
orchestration of music to the spheres,
complementing all. Such it is with I, created as thee
in earth for all to see.

The leaves are there in you, and I, the love you
feel, am the wind, blowing with your soul to open
wide the door of heaven's keeping.

And every plane to which I send Myself in you
will be your home and that experience to which is
Mine, and I shall enjoy that which is the sublime—
the joy of the Lord, as you keep it in your mind.

Each of us, that which is the Love I am, serving One in another one is the keeper of the flame, and the eye that I see through you is the eye that sees through the other one. Recognize this is what is called, 'coming home.'

I am programmed by the Love I am, and you are that. I am impulsed by the Love I am, and you are that. Love moves love, expanded always, embracing more of love. As I choose to choose that which is chosen as impulsed love and wisdom, I accept My Divinity, and I am made known unto Myself. Herein am I glorified, My Beloved One, and in the end as in the beginning, the all is a beginning again—more Love expressed.

I Am the Will of God,
And the gift out of that possession
will feed a multitude;
And the gift out of that wisdom will heal the sick;
And the gift out of that vibration
will transform hearts,
And Peace will be the gift.

The Love which is Mine, is yours,
And that which is yours is Mine.

You have no power other than My Will.
You have no mind other than My Will.
You have no Love other than My Will.
Life is My Will,
And the gift which is the gift in My Will
Is the image of God I am you are.

Opulent universes within worlds supply the need and the demand of My universes created from within Myself. Each species of I-dentities carries forth My name expressing realm to realm, universe to universe, world to world—connected as a spider's web. Movement within the web itself, at any juncture, creates movement in the entirety of the whole. Therefore, remember, Beloved One, your Love is the movement of My Love and affects the whole. How important then am I within Myself you are?

Present not anything less than Love in the earth. Accept not anything less than Love in your mind. Receive not anything less than Love in your heart. Extend not anything less than Love in your life. Love is the immune system of all disease. Light is the Source of all love. I am the Source of Light, and you are that.

My offerings are through your hands.
Your eyes and your voice are My commands,
Sacred as the covenant, the Holy Grail,
The pearl so long sought is now unveiled.

Awake, oh sleeper, My child of Light.
A new Earth is born in you this day.
As you step forward in My Earth,
You will know that I,
The you, you are, I am,
Created Earth for Myself to explore—
Indeed, a journey of love.

I am the stories of old
And the stories yet to come.
I am the high-rise and the new beginning.
I am the earth, the fire, the air,
The water, and the sea,
All mixed together are one in Me—
Forever, eternally.

Each element created I in earth.
And far, far regions beyond this one,
Yet to be explored, My Beloved One.
Be the Love I am remembered,
For you already be the Love I am.
Be it now remembered.

I Am the Love, the Peace, and the Joy.
I am the gift of the Word of God
And the Life made flesh in all.
I am the Spirit from on High,
And I am that which gifts One
with the understanding of the mind.

I differentiate Myself
To experience all that I can be,
And you, My Beloved,
Are remembering Me.

Watch Me walk in the footsteps
Of the animal kingdom as well,
In the birds that fly o'er Earth,
And the fish that swim in the sea—
'Tis Me.

You are the journey in the journey, journeying, and I am that. What a journey I am taking each step you take. Your sojourn is My pleasure and My passion. So, Beloved One, wouldst thou not bless I that am you by enjoying the journey? Indeed. Return now to your life with an awareness that it is Mine, and as I am enjoyed herein, am I fulfilled.

Master teachers blend their Light,
And I am Master teacher in all.
And when you feel the need to call
The Master teacher to your side,
Recognize 'tis I, indeed.
And I, as you, am supplied
As Master teacher of all.

*Master is a term your mind can understand.
Beyond the Master is the Presence which the
Master seeks to know, and here is where we begin
the Revelation in the new world to come—not to be
the Master, but the Presence I Am. From this point
then, you will create according to what is given
in the Presence—not seeking to know, but known;
not seeking to find, not seeking to understand,
not seeking to believe—just I Am. As I Am is,
then, so shall it be, and that which is to become is
experienced, eventually, by what is even more of
itself to begin again and again.*

What search is needed to One
Who is found?
Instead, the pleasure of Holy ground
Beneath your feet I stand,
Renowned.

And in the beginning as in the end,
The all is a beginning again–
More Love expressed.

Essence Speaks,
Love to All, I Am,
Diadra

Diadra is the co-founder, along with her husband, John Price, of *Wings of Spirit* ™, a not-for-profit foundation dedicated to expanding awareness and awakening the destiny of the human Spirit from within the heart of humanity.

For speaking engagements, workshops, and retreats, contact:

Wings of Spirit ™
P.O. Box 285
Blowing Rock, NC 28605

Phone: (828) 265-4017
Fax: (828) 263-0101
e-mail: wings@wingsofspirit.com
website: www.wings-of-spirit.org/

145902